MARCO ⊕ POLO

Travel with **Insider**

77.

LIBRARIES
LEABHARLANNA

CORK CITY COUNCIL | COMHAIRLE CATHRACH CHORCAÍ

You can renew items through the online catalogue at
www.corkcitylibraries.ie, or by telephone.
Please return this item on time as others may be waiting for it.
Overdue charges: 50c per notice + 30c per week.

Is féidir iasachtaí a athnuachan trí bhíthin na catalóige ag
www.corkcitylibraries.ie, nó ar an nguthán.
Muna gcuirtear iasacht ar ais in am, gearrfar costaisí
50c do gach fógra, maraon le 30c in aghaidh na seachtaine.

Class no./Ur. aicme: ___915.97 MAR___

Tory Top Library
Leabharlann Bhóthar na mBuaircíní
021 4924934/46
torytop_library@corkcity.ie

D1362677

SYMBOLS

INSIDER TIP	Insider Tip
★	Highlight
●●●●	Best of ...
☼	Scenic view
☺	Responsible travel: fair trade principles and the environment respected
(*)	Telephone numbers that are not toll-free

PRICE CATEGORIES HOTELS

Expensive over 2,700,000 dong

Moderate 675,000 – 2,700,000 dong

Budget under 675,000 dong

The prices given are minimum prices for a double room per night

PRICE CATEGORIES RESTAURANTS

Expensive over 270,000 dong

Moderate 100,000 – 270,000 dong

Budget under 100,000 dong

The prices are for one meal per person without drinks

On the cover: A Robinson Crusoe paradise p. 98 | Amazing dripstone caves p. 108

DISCOVER VIETNAM!

'Bonjour, madame.' The old monk bows hesitantly, as if in slow motion, at the same time removing the wine-red woolly cap from his bald head. In his wrinkled hand a visiting card bearing the greeting 'Happy New Year'. Emerging from behind his hunched Methuselah back a Mohican-style tuft of hair. The novice stoops to present a *chom chom*, a hairy, red rambutan fruit. Normally it's the visitors who offer gifts here, not the monks, but no one expects any sacrificial offerings from foreigners – sometimes they rush in and, after a flurry of camera flashlights, quickly disappear; the Buddhas and the monks take it all in their stride. Wind chimes tinkle in the breeze that blows through the hallowed halls. Breathe deep, at last here's somewhere away from the clatter of mopeds and the cacophony of hooting cars, a place to pause, a place for a dialogue with Buddha.

Welcome to Vietnam. A country moving swiftly into the 21st century. Moss and a patina shroud monuments thousands of years old, but on the streets of Saigon and Hanoi the modern world is everywhere, leaving new arrivals rubbing their eyes

Photo: Ha Long Bay

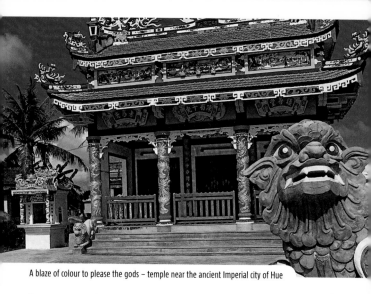

A blaze of colour to please the gods – temple near the ancient Imperial city of Hue

in amazement. A country leaving the past behind, moving away from the clichés associated with the Vietnam War, opium pipes and snake wine. Today's travellers are taken aback by the species-rich national parks and natural treasures, from the Unesco-protected Ha Long Bay in the north to the amphibian world of the Mekong Delta in the far south. In between, some 3,200km (2,000mi) of coastline dotted with islands, beaches and remote hideaways. In the cities, beside broad, tamarind-shaded avenues, colourful Chinese temples sit comfortably alongside colonial mansions and weather-worn villas in shades of soft ochre. At the same time the skyline rises higher with every blink of the eye.

Mopeds, mopeds everywhere – this is most people's first impression of the country. They often just emerge like swarms of bees, laden with boxes full of cola bottles or Tiger beer, bulging shopping bags, chicken cages, and weighed down with two or three children, betel-chewing old men or women in fluttering ao dai gowns and

wearing white gloves to protect against the sun and the dirt.

Vietnam can look back proudly on 4,000 years of history, but few other countries have suffered so painfully from wars and foreign rule by the Chinese, the French, the Japanese and finally the Americans. The same nationalities are returning, but this time they come in peace. About 6 million visitors and impressive annual growth rates are spreading prosperity among the Vietnamese. This southeast Asian country is booming, and not only as a travel destination. Most of the 87 million Vietnamese people moved on long ago from the devastating Vietnam War; two thirds of all inhabitants are under 35 years of age and only know about it from history books. Holidaymakers can now safely give the Ho Chi Minh trail and the Viet Cong tunnels a miss – Vietnam

has much more to offer. Now travellers can go on journeys of discovery wherever they please. It could be to the enchanting pagoda around the corner wafting with scented smoke, the bustling fruit market with rambutan and melon sellers, butchers, Chinese traders advertising their fabrics and pots and pans with dramatic gestures, to idyllic unspoilt beaches with no sun beds or parasols. They may even feel up to negotiating the semi-organised mayhem on the sometimes badly pot-holed roads.

> **Wherever there's a *tay*, there's always something to laugh about**

And then there's this friendly, sometimes mischievous curiosity. Wherever there's a tay, a Westerner, there's always something happening, something to laugh about. They do well from selling something to the *tay* and, it's true, a few travellers regard their methods as intrusive. But if you don't react to their sales pitch, most traders quickly lose interest. Children try out their English and shout 'I love you' or 'Hello mister!'. In larger towns everyone is, of course, very polite; they are masters in observing the proprieties. Respect for others, especially one's elders, is considered a virtue; it's a Confucian commandment, together with ancestor worship and hard work. Often up to three generations live in one room, so that could easily be seven or eight people. An apartment, a little house? Unthinkable on modest wages. A woman working in a factory will take home six to nine dollars a day, if she is prepared to work for up to 14 hours mixing noodle dough, pressing moulds or sorting screws. Living space in Saigon has become unaffordable; the few available plots of land, homes or apartments change hands very quickly for the equivalent of many hundreds of thousands of dollars.

Important values – hard work, respect and ancestor worship

Welcome to turbo-capitalism! Doi Moi, who in 1986 introduced the communist government's economic reforms, has transformed Vietnamese society. Profit is a new word in the vocabulary. The average annual income is estimated at around 1,200 US$. In the last two decades poverty has more than halved, but the urban-rural divide is still great. While the largest ethnic minority, the Chinese, dominate the business world, especially in the cities of southern Vietnam, most of the country's 54 ethnic groups live in the mountains and in the central highlands. These minorities are still in the transitional phase between a life revolving around ancient traditions and the digital era. Each group wears its own costumes, celebrates its own festivals and follows its own customs (such as a belief in natural spirits, houses on stilts, betel-nut chewing, tooth blackening).

The 'Vietnamese Alps' and the Imperial city of Hue

Vietnam's scenic beauty is enchanting. In the tropical southern zones, the pattern is damp, sultry summers and warm winters, whereas in the sub-tropical north the climate is more familiar to Europeans, i.e. hot summers, but cooler, wet winters. Many are taken aback by Ha Long Bay with its towering limestone rocks and darkly shimmering water, but also the breathtakingly rugged 'Vietnamese Alps' in the northwest,

1976 (2 July)
The Socialist Republic of Vietnam is founded

2000
Trading agreement with the United States. President Bill Clinton visits Vietnam. Severe flooding in the Mekong Delta

2005
Opening of the 6.3km (3.9mi) Hai Van tunnel between Da Nang and Hue

2007
Vietnam becomes a member of the World Trade Organisation

2008/2009
After the economic miracle (from 1991), the world financial crisis hits Vietnam.

Vietnam's daily bread – farmers harvesting rice

which can even get a covering of snow in cold winters. With its Palace of Supreme Harmony and royal tombs, the old Imperial city of Hue on the Perfume River is impressive. Near Phan Thiet warm sand crunches underfoot on the beach at Mui Ne, Saigon with its renovated colonial buildings now looks much smarter and in the Mekong Delta the chugging engines of the long-tail boats provide an ever-present background beat.

The whole experience is topped off with a wide range of Vietnamese delicacies and a perfect holiday schedule of swimming, diving, windsurfing, sailing or walking in one of the country's 25 or so national parks. Whether you are hanging upside down from rocks, attempting to climb a limestone pillar in Ha Long Bay, joining in slow-motion tai chi exercises, squinting through the incense smoke of a pagoda or feeling overwhelmed on your bike in the chaotic congestion of Hanoi, eventually you will get closer to the Vietnamese, their ubiquitous dragons and mysterious spirits. There's no question about it – a trip to Vietnam is an adventure for all the senses.

In its wake come inflation, collapse of the property and stock market and devaluation of the dong

2010
Hanoi is 1,000 years old – a spectacular celebration on 10.10.10 commemorates the event

2011
Vietnam reaches Middle Income Status (1,000 US$ per capita) largely as a result of continuing high growth, with GDP growth averaging 6.9% over the previous five years. Work on improving Saigon's transport network starts. Metro due for completion in 2015, plans for an expressway put to tender

WHAT'S HOT

1

Eat ethically

Hanoi with a big heart In Hanoi's teaching restaurants disadvantaged teenagers are being trained as chefs, restaurant managers or waiters. If you would like to lend your support to this project, then dine at *Song Thu*. Don't worry! The food is excellent *(34 Châu Long street)*. The non-profit restaurant *Koto* has adopted a similar approach. They also run cookery classes for tourists *(59 Van Mieu street)* and *Baguette & Chocolate* is training young people in several of its stores *(in the Museum of Ethnology, Nguyen Van Huyen)*.

A rich heritage

2

Fashion *Mhin Hanh* embellishes her clothing with silk and embroidery *(24 Dong Khoi, Saigon, photo)*, *Ipa Nima* adorns handbags with mother-of-pearl, etc. *(73 Trang Thi street, Hanoi)*, and the young team at *Konheo* are running riot with a range of fun t-shirts *(32 Dinh Tien Hoang, Saigon)*. In a nutshell, the fashion scene in Vietnam is flourishing. The design world keeps up-to-date at the *Dep Fashion Show (www.depfashion.com)*.

Get on your board

3

Get paddling With or without wind. Water sports enthusiasts get good value for their money off the Vietnam coast – especially around Mui Ne. If the wind drops, on a stand-up paddle board; when the wind's blowing, kite surfing. Whatever the weather, Rob Kidnie of *Kite'n'Surf* is on hand to give guidance. Equipment can be hired from the professionals too *(64–66 Nguyen Dinh Chieu street, www. kite-n-surf.com)*. Alternatively, the *Storm Kite Center (24 Nguyen Dinh Chieu street, www.stormkiteboarding.com)* may be able to help. Failing that, try the *Windchimes windsurfing* school *(56 Nguyen Dinh Chieu street, www.kiteboarding-vietnam.com)*.

Independent art

Going solo It's all happening in the art world. More and more mini-galleries are opening, and this is helping new artists to get a foot in the door. Tucked away in courtyards or old industrial buildings, the art world is alive and well. *San Art* is run by artists for artists. The programme of events includes temporary exhibitions with works by the young and creative, as well as discussion groups and lectures by foreign artists, some of whom are invited to attend art events or become 'resident artists' *(3 Me Linh, Saigon, www.san-art. org)*. The *Mai Gallery* can offer more exhibition space for the next generation. It represents some big names, so it has the facilities to exhibit works by less well-known artists, such as Dang Xuan Hoa *(113 Hang Bong St, Hanoi, www.dangxu anhoagallery.com, photo)*.

In tune with the times

Nha Tho This is where the capital's heart beats. Nha Tho street is the place for Hanoi's fashion-conscious connoisseur. City life is played out in the area around the cathedral, in cafés, such as the *Paris Deli*. Get a seat on the balcony and watch the hustle and bustle below *(13 Nha Tho)*. Shoppers will also find a wide range of stores in this street. In *Mosaique*, for example, which doesn't have the usual paraphernalia, but high-quality interior design and souvenirs with a difference *(22 Nha Tho, www.mosaiquedecoration.com, photo)*. If you feel like staying around, then check into the cool *Church Hotel (9 Nha Tho, www. churchhotel.com.vn)*.

IN A NUTSHELL

ANCESTOR WORSHIP

For the Vietnamese, family ties do not end with death; deceased family members can still positively influence the fortunes of the living. For these ties to continue, the dead must be supplied, at least symbolically, with food and money. For this reason, many houses and temples have small altars serving as focal points for ancestor worship. On the anniversary of a loved one's death, during religious holidays and at family banquets, sweets, fruit or cigarettes, for example, are left as offerings.

ART AND CRAFTS

In the 11th century crafts and painting flourished in Vietnam. Popular artists painted peasant scenes, such as the rice harvest or the planting out. Entire communities were involved in making black-and-white woodcuts, now known as tranh tet or New Year pictures. At the same time, the Than Hoa School of the Ly dynasty (1009–1225) was producing probably the country's finest ceramics, pottery which was much admired even in Japan and China. In the 13th century artists discovered the art of silk painting and set about creating, among other things, portraits used for ancestor worship. The Cham culture with its Buddhist and Hindu figures brought about a revival in sculpture and woodcarving skills. In the 15th century painting with lacquer, a technique which had existed in China for many centuries, became fashionable. Today, hundreds of painters earn a living

Photo: Thien Hau Pagoda in Saigon

The Vietnamese work hard, from early morning until late at night, sustained by superstition and miracle healing

from copying artworks. Works by Picasso or Rembrandt can be seen hanging on every street corner in Hanoi's Old Quarter, of course, only as inexpensive replicas of the famous masters' oeuvres. You could pick up a Caravaggio or a Dali for approx. 1,000,000 dong.

CHAM MINORITY

You are most likely to encounter the Cham in south-central Vietnam. Between the 4th and 13th centuries, Champa, the kingdom of their forefathers, was one of the most powerful empires in southeast Asia, extending well into what is now Cambodia. Of the 250 temple sites that once belonged to the Cham civilisation only 20 ruins now remain, one of which is the Unesco World Heritage Site at My Son near Da Nang *(see p. 63)*. The architecture and symbolism (such as the lingam, a phallic symbol for the Hindu god Shiva) clearly show that the early Cham were Hindus. Their successors, however, of whom about 100,000 are still living in Vietnam, follow the Islamic faith, but it is a very moderate version with its own festivals. The Cham Museum in Da Nang *(see p. 61)* offers an excellent insight into Cham culture.

CONFUCIANISM

For almost 2,000 years, Confucianism has been the prevailing ethical and political philosophy in Vietnam. Created by the Chinese philosopher Confucius 2,500 years ago, it defines the relationships and code of conduct within the family and society, even within the state structure. The young are subordinate to their elders, women to men, subjects to their ruler. The five most important virtues are 'humaneness', loyalty to one's true nature, reciprocity, filial piety and virtue. In everyday relationships, the teachings of Confucianism are ever-present, especially in families. They determine the ranking of individual family members – the oldest male is always the most respected person. This also applies to social interactions. So don't be surprised if the first question you are asked is your age!

ECONOMY

In 2007 Vietnam joined the World Trade Organization (WTO). The economic boom that the country has enjoyed since 1991 (7–8 per cent growth per year) is also attributable to the thousands of expatriate Vietnamese returning to their homeland to establish joint venture businesses, mainly in the prosperous south. Industry, construction, the service sector and exports have seen the largest share of growth. Probably the most important sectors here are the automotive, motorcycle, steel and cement sectors, as well as tourism and banking. The main exports include crude oil, textiles and footwear, seafood and rice. In 2010 Gross Domestic Product stood at around 1,200 US$ per capita, but with a significant urban-rural divide. Like the Chinese, the Vietnamese are masters at copying. They take the copyright concept literally. For them it means *'the right to copy'*. Millions of illegally-copied DVDs are sourced in Vietnam.

Built in memory of 'Uncle Ho' – the Ho Chi Minh Museum in Hanoi

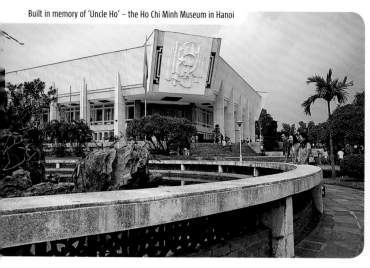

FAUNA AND FLORA

Big cats, including leopards, tigers and civets, roam the Vietnamese jungles. But in the forests there are also elephants, bears, jackals, skunk, mongoose, flying squirrels and deer. No more than 12 percent of the country is tropical forest, mainly in the south, and as many as 1,500 different tree species grow there. And then there are 800 different bird species, crocodiles, pythons and various lizards, as well as rare monkeys, including the eastern black crested gibbon, which until 2002 was thought to be extinct. In the north tropical deciduous forests flourish. At higher altitudes evergreen mountain forest predominates, while in the flat coastal regions to the north and south of the country there are mangrove forests. The use of chemical agents during the Vietnam War and also forest clearances have seriously damaged the original vegetation.

HO CHI MINH

Even as a young revolutionary Ho Chi Minh fought against French colonial rule, which dated from 1862/63, and in Hong Kong in 1930 he founded the Communist Party of Vietnam. When the country was partitioned in 1954, he became president of the Democratic Republic of Vietnam, usually called North Vietnam. In July 1976, the country was reunited as the Socialist Republic of Vietnam, but it was not an event the still-revered 'Uncle Ho' witnessed. He died on 2 September 1969 at the age of 79.

POPULATION

Vietnam has a population of 87 million, but ethnically it is a 'melting pot'. About 88 percent of the population belong to the largest ethnic group, the Viet (also known as Kinh). There are 53 distinct ethnic minorities, the largest groups, each one about a million strong, being the hill tribes (the Tay and Muong), the ethnic Chinese Hoa and the Cambodian Khmer, with the latter clustered in the Mekong Delta. But the hill tribes still differ significantly in their traditions, language, dress, festivals and settlement patterns. The Vietnamese often call the hill tribes moi (savages). Each ethnic group lives independently and there is hardly any intermarriage. Incidentally, in Indochina and beyond, the Vietnamese are regarded as the 'Germans of Asia'. Thanks to their appetite for hard work and an ability to improvise, they survived not only the war and the years of austerity which followed, but also within just a few years transformed a napalm-scorched land into one of the world's top rice exporters.

POLITICAL SYSTEM

In 1954, after the First Indochina War against the French, the Geneva Conference ruled that Vietnam should be divided into the Democratic Republic of Vietnam in the north and the southern half within the US sphere of influence (a 'temporary' partitioning of the country). After the Vietnam War in 1976 the country was reunited as the Socialist Republic of Vietnam. The formal head of state is the president who is elected by parliament every five years; Truong Tan Sang was elected to the office in 2011. At the head of the government's Council of Ministers is Prime Minister Nguyen Tan Dung, a reformer. The 498 members of the National Assembly, mostly members of the Communist Party (CP), are elected for five years and formally monitor the work of government. Policy is set by the General Secretary of the Communist Party (since 2011 Nguyen Phu Trong). The government continues to take a tough line with its critics. Fighting corruption and crime are important objectives. In 2004 mafia boss Nam Cam and five of his henchmen were executed.

RELIGION

Religious and animistic beliefs co-exist peacefully in the temples and pagodas of Vietnam. For thousands of years, Chinese philosophy, as preached by the Buddha, Lao Tse and Confucius, as well as more recently the teachings of Jesus Christ, have had a role to play in everyday life. It is not a problem for a Vietnamese person to be both a Buddhist and a Christian.

Within Buddhism there are two basic directions: the Theravada (also called Hinayana) Buddhists and the Mahayana Buddhists. It is the latter who prevail in Vietnam. Both seek salvation and perfection through infinite patience, compassion and tolerance towards all living beings.

There is no proof that Lao Tse actually existed; in fact many of his followers see him as a mythical figure, who drew various threads together to define what we now call Taoism. The philosophy emphasises harmony, contemplation and simplicity, as achieved through the Tao or The Way. Key symbols are the Vietnamese equivalents of yin and yang, complementary opposites, unseen (hidden, feminine) and seen (manifest, masculine), with Jade Emperor Ngoc Hoang as the supreme 'Ruler of Heaven'.

Approx. 1–2 million Vietnamese are members of the Cao Dai cult, which was founded in 1926. The Cao Dai pope stands at the head of this fusion of major religions, supplemented by a pinch of the occult (séances), mysticism and the cult of celebrity involving much-revered, but now deceased representatives from politics and world literature. Most of the 500 or so rather colourful Cao Dai temples are to be found in the south.

RICE

The cultivation of rice, one of the country's main agricultural products, employs around two-thirds of the population. It would be hard to imagine the daily routine without rice, a crop the Vietnamese have been growing for thousands of years. Many of the country's myths and legends have grown up around rice. Vietnam is now among the world's top three rice-exporting nations. Some 3 million people in the Mekong Delta alone work as rice farmers. This is where the highest rice yields occur, since the water in the Mekong rises and falls regularly, thus creating optimum conditions for the irrigation of the paddies, which can provide up to three harvests per year.

SPECIAL 'DELICACIES'

Vietnamese cuisine is very varied and there will be treats to suit all tastes on the dining table (see 'Food & Drink', p. 24). But the 'specialities' can include certain items that are unfamiliar and Westerners would find them repulsive. But superstition is widespread. Here men, usually of Chinese descent, will eat a virility-enhancing tiger penis, turtle eggs for a long life or a bird's nest soup. Other delicacies include 'warming' dog (in the colder north), boiled monkey brains, snake meat, civets, frogs, etc. But don't worry. Such dishes are expensive – the locals would never offer them to an ignorant 'long nose', as Europeans are called.

SUPERSTITION

Local superstitions often seem to have grown out of a strange combination of Taoist ideas – such as unlucky days or ill omens – and earth religion. Evidence of this can be found in temples, where slips of papers marked with

The Water Puppet Theatre – popular entertainment for hundreds of years

distorted Chinese characters are burnt in order to symbolically eradicate evil spirits. More and more self-proclaimed prophets move between villages, resolving family squabbles, reconciling quarrelsome lovers or preparing horoscopes. Miracle healers are also in demand, mixing strange concoctions to cure all kinds of complaints.

VIETNAM WAR

The Vietnamese prefer not to talk about the past. This mindset corresponds to a degree with the Taoist belief that if you constantly rake over tragic events, in the end you are inviting history to repeat itself. But it is impossible to ignore the fact that the war led to the death and injury of over 4 million people, the devastation of huge swathes of land, villages and towns, not to mention terrible massacres such as the one at My Lai. Between 1964 and 1975, the Americans waged an unprecedented war against the communist forces of the Viet Cong. The Cold War, between the US-led western world on one side and Soviet-led communism on the other, was being played out in earnest in this small corner of the globe, with the Vietnamese people being the main victims. Only after the visit to Vietnam by US President Bill Clinton Vietnam, 25 years after the victory of the Viet Cong, were relations between the two former adversaries normalised.

WATER PUPPETS

The art of water puppetry was developed by rice farmers as a form of entertainment during breaks in their often back-breaking work. The puppets, made from fig tree wood, were modelled on villagers, animals, mythical creatures or spirits. They were often mounted on a floating 'stage' and then activated from below the water level with a bamboo stick. Performances depicted scenes from everyday life, events from the village or in the fields. Today's puppets are usually over 50cm (20ins) tall and can weigh up to 15kg (30lb), so considerable strength and skill are required. The art was revived when the Municipal Water Puppet Theatre in Hanoi was opened.

FOOD & DRINK

Tu Duc, the fourth emperor of the Nguyen dynasty, who ruled the country from Hue between 1847 and 1883, had a passion for fine food. At every meal he wanted 50 dishes, prepared by 50 chefs and served by 50 waiters.

The kitchen staff did their utmost to comply with his wishes... and that's the reason why traditional Vietnamese cuisine boasts over 500 different dishes.

All the dishes you order – meat, fish and seafood, eggs, vegetables, salads and soups – are served at the same time, plus of course *com trang* or boiled rice. On the table will be plates with finely chopped vegetables or fresh herbs, such as basil, coriander, parsley, mint or lemon grass, which can be scattered over the dishes as required; lettuce leaves are also of-

ten included. Also, small but very good baguettes are served everywhere, a legacy of Vietnam's French colonial masters. Rice noodles or egg noodles are mainly included in soup (*bun* or *pho*). One variation could be *mien luon,* a noodle soup with chunks of eel. Wherever you go, you will find *mien ga,* a noodle soup with chicken, mushrooms, shallots or vegetables. A large bottle of *nuoc mam,* the fish sauce made in factories in Phan Thiet and on the island of Phu Quoc, is a standard condiment and should be sprinkled liberally on every dish. The meal opens with the words *xin moi* (please tuck in), whereupon everyone takes their chopsticks to fill their rice bowl and starts eating. Restaurant choices range from fine dining to small, roadside food stalls. In up-

Plain rice or a colourful fruit platter – whatever you choose, you will have to learn how to balance those delicious morsels on your chopsticks

market restaurants you will find western-style à la carte menus. In fact, in many hotel restaurants chefs pander too much to the perceived preferences of western diners. Hot flavours are toned down and a lot of fats are used. The many speciality restaurants in the major cities and tourist areas, however, are often excellent – proper gourmet eateries serving authentic dishes in a sophisticated ambience. Because of the cooler climate in the north, the emphasis tends to be more on braised, deep-fried and pan-

fried dishes, and also on rice porridge. In the emperor's heartlands around Hue, the people eat accordingly: a number of restaurants geared towards tourism there specialise in the dishes once favoured by the Imperial court, so the food is not just splendidly garnished, piquantly seasoned, but also appetisingly presented. If you are in Hue, then you are sure to see *banh khoai* on the menu: crispy pancakes with prawns, pork, bean sprouts and a sauce made from peanuts and sesame seeds.

LOCAL SPECIALITIES

▶ **Banh cuon** – steamed, wafer-thin rice cake with minced meat

▶ **Bon bay mon** – beef in wafer-thin slices, marinated in various sauces, a Saigon speciality

▶ **Bun cha** – chargrilled pork patties

▶ **Bun thang** – hearty soup with rice noodles, chicken and pork, prawns and fried eggs (photo right)

▶ **Canh chua** – sweet and sour fish soup, heavily seasoned with tamarind, coriander and bean sprouts

▶ **Cha** – finely sliced marinated pork, chargrilled

▶ **Cha ca** – finely chopped fish fillets marinated in fish sauce and saffron, threaded on to wooden skewers and grilled

▶ **Cha gio** – spring roll, usually made with thin rice pastry, filled with prawns, pork, egg, noodles and mushrooms, then fried in oil. National dish, known as *nem ran* in the north (photo left)

▶ **Com thap cam** – fried rice with chicken, pork, sausages, egg yolk, carrots, peas, ginger and other spices

▶ **Dua gia** – pickled bean sprout salad

▶ **Ech tam bot ran** – frog meat in batter, fried in oil; served with vinegar, pepper and fish sauce

▶ **Ga kho gung** – chicken boiled with ginger, fish sauce, sugar and pepper, caramelised (south Vietnam)

▶ **Gio** – lean pork, crushed in a mortar, then wrapped in banana leaves and boiled

▶ **Hot pot** – a kind of Vietnamese fondue: fish, seafood, beef, glass noodles cooked in a simmering stock in a samovar or clay pot at the table Plus onions, tomatoes, mushrooms, beans and other vegetables

▶ **Mam chung** – fermented fish (from the rice paddy), very aromatic, stuffed and steamed with minced meat, egg, noodles and herbs

In the south, more exotic, sometimes fiery, ingredients find their way into the pots and pans. The mixture is stirred briskly, sautéed briefly, grilled and seasoned generously, sometimes with hot spices in curry style.

But no trip to Vietnam is complete without sampling the fare at one of the wayside food stalls. You can usually get a tasty soup or a stew for between 10,000 and 20,000 dong. Outside the main cities look out for restaurants advertising *com pho* (rice soup). Few people speak

English in the rural areas, so ask to see the price written down.

Visitors to Vietnam are often advised to get some practice in using chopsticks. You can always ask for a knife and fork, but it's much more fun to 'do as the Romans do' and that means holding the two sticks delicately between thumb, forefinger and middle finger. Please note: the superstitious Vietnamese believe that chopsticks should never be left standing upright in your bowl. This gesture is used to honour deceased family members. It is impolite to poke around in the food, it's better to just pick out individual morsels. And pointing at people with chopsticks is also considered to be bad manners.

You will find many different kinds of delicious desserts in Vietnam. *Banh bao* are a good example. These are small, sweet dumplings filled with meat and vegetables. *Banh deo* are sticky rice cakes soaked in sugar water and filled with fruit and sesame seeds. *Banh it nhan dao,* cakes made from mung bean starch, rice flour and sugar, are steamed in banana leaves. If you fancy candied fruit — it could be fruit or vegetables — then order *mut.* Usually served with Vietnamese tea are sugar-sweet, jellied mung bean cake, known as banh dau xan, and as a speciality for Tet, the Vietnamese New Year festival, it has to be *banh chung,* sticky rice cakes filled with beans and meat.

The fruit selection is seemingly endless. Incidentally, you will often see fruit used as sacrificial offerings in temples, but each one has a particular symbolism: a coconut, for example, stands for frugality, a papaya for pleasure, a cherimoya fulfils a wish, plums are for longevity, the dragon fruit gives strength, and the 'eyes of the dragon' *(longans, similar to lychees)* are said to have a relaxing effect. Quench your thirst with mineral water

(nuoc soi), but if you prefer something sweet, then you will have no problem finding all kinds of colas and soft drinks. But do not overlook drinks such as the ubiquitous green tea *(che),* fresh coconut milk *(nuoc dua)* or the tasty tropical fruit juices *(sinh to).* Rice wine may not be to

You must give them a try – snacks from a street stall

everyone's taste, but few people could dislike the beer – either as a *bia hoi* (draft beer) as Castel, Huda (from Hue), Saigon Export, Bia Hanoi, Salida or 333 (say *ba ba ba)* – and at 15,000 dong a glass very affordable.

Vietnamese coffee is very good and very strong. When coffee is served, placed on top of the cup will be a special metal filter and ground coffee. Boiling water is then poured on to the coffee, which drains through into the cup containing a generous quantity of condensed milk.

SHOPPING

Vietnam is heaven for souvenir hunters. The shops you visit will have a wide range of goods, but no price tags. That's because you will have to negotiate a price. Take your time over the deal and you will probably come away with a bargain. The antiques are always interesting, but sellers can often conveniently forget that tourists need an export licence to take a piece of wood out of the country. Without this permit, the goods will be confiscated when you pass through customs – even imitation antiques. And another thing to remember: jewels are often cheap fakes.

ARTS AND CRAFTS

Silk, hand-painted or printed cotton fabrics, embroidery, copper and silver objets d'art, jewellery, statues, wood carvings, miniatures, leather goods, carpets and even beautiful furniture with inlays are available at reasonable prices. If you are on your way from Hanoi to Ha Long City, then you really should stop off at the *Hong Ngoc Humanity Center (on the N 18 | Sao Do, Hai Duong)*. The goods on sale here include shoes, silk garments, tea sets, books and paintings, with the proceeds going towards a training project for people with disabilities. How about a statue of Ho Chi Minh in white marble for the ter-

race at home or a lime green Buddha as a paperweight? At the foot of the Marble Mountains in the village of Quang Nam, master sculptors are kept hard at work – you can hear the unmistakeable hammering of chisels from up in the mountains. Not far from the centre of Nha Trang, south of Hon Chong Bay, the Hong Chau Sa family specialises in producing paintings from 30 different natural shades of sand. You will find some unusual souvenirs here, such as Ho Chi Minh's face, a typical Vietnamese landscape or, especially for customers from the west, Santa Claus. *(4 B Nha Tho | Vinh Hai, Nha Trang).*

CLOTHING

In the silk shops, such as those in 'tailor town', Hoi An, you can have practically anything made to measure and in your choice of fabric, all at very affordable prices. If you would like an ao dai, the national dress for Vietnamese women, you can get a nice one for around 500,000 dong, but do bear in mind that these silk garments are really intended for warmer climate zones.

CONICAL HATS

The traditional conical hats are worn by the rice farmers as protection against rain or

From elaborately-decorated straw hats to tailor-made silk blouses – you will find some great gifts in Vietnam

sun. If you want a good quality hat, you will find thin scraps of paper between the lengths of straw. The finest cone hats come from the Hue region. Phu Cam (also known as Phuoc Vinh), the hatters' village, lies on the south bank of the An Cuu river. Here, the women deploy skills acquired over the generations to produce semi-translucent hats made from palm leaves, which they decorate with silk thread, images of the landscape or lines of poetry (also available in the Dong Ba market in Hue.

LACQUERWARE

The resin of the son tree is collected and made into a brown or black lacquer, which is then used to decorate accessories and home ware, anything from a tea set to lounge suites. If you are considering a more expensive piece in a specialist store, ask INSIDER TIPP how many paint layers were applied. The more layers there are, the more expensive the item. Ten is the minimum number, the maximum could be more than 100.

PHOTOGRAPHS

One of the best Vietnamese photographers is Thanh Long. You can buy his pictures in poster format at his INSIDER TIPP gallery in Nha Trang. Common themes are evocative studies of everyday life with a remarkable, sometimes disturbing interplay between light and shade. *126 Hoang Van Thu | Nha Trang | www.longthanhart.com*

POP MUSIC

The range of cheap CDs and music cassettes is huge. Fusion is the current fad. Huong Thanh ('Dragonfly') is a popular exponent of the genre and her voice is quite gentle; Vietnam's most popular singer, Than Lam, produces a much more powerful sound. Jazz guitarist Nguyen Le is renowned for his western-inspired, traditional music. Ethno-jazz performer Billy Bang ('The Aftermath') has a devoted following.

THE PERFECT ROUTE

FROM THE METROPOLIS TO THE BEACH

Take the N 1 from ❶ *Saigon* → p. 81 past seemingly endless suburban sprawl as far as the coast. Make your first stop in the port city of ❷ *Phan Thiet* → p. 95 with its fine, 20-km (12-mi) long beach on the ❸ *Mui Ne peninsula* → p. 96. After the traffic chaos of Saigon, this place is a haven of peace and tranquillity. Amateur photographers in search of artistic shots will be inspired by the famous sand dunes here.

THROUGH THE CHAM REGION

As you proceed north, do stop off near the bustling town of *Phan Rang* to see the remarkable Cham towers at ❹ *Po Klong Garai* → p. 59, which date from the 13/14th century. You will encounter the impressive legacy of this once powerful tribe later. As you continue along the N 1 coast road, stop off for a swim in the sea near ❺ *Nha Trang* → p. 92, Vietnam's first beach resort (photo above). Former emperor Bao Dai used to take a dip here. If you like to go in a little deeper, then there are some worthwhile things for you to do. It may be something for another time, but there are no fewer than 25 dive sites and 70 offshore islands to explore. Take a break from the beach with its hawkers and campfire parties and pay a visit to the Long Son Pagoda, where the enormous white Buddha is the main attraction.

KEEP TO THE COAST

Keep to the coast on the spectacular mountain pass near Dai Lanh and enjoy some amazing views. The mountains gradually get closer to the coast, until finally the city of *Qui Nhon* comes into view. Stay the night in one of the new beach hotels here or carry on to ❻ *Hoi An* → p. 64 (photo below). Once a small fishing town on the Thu Bon river, it has now a very popular spot with travellers. In recent years, dozens of hotels in all price categories have opened here to satisfy demand. Souvenir shops, galleries and tailors quickly followed. It is definitely worth spending time here to admire the beautiful old timber buildings, trading houses, Chinese pagodas and covered bridges. There's also a beach...

A LITTLE BIT OF HISTORY AND THE CLOUD PASS

It's only a short hop to ❼ *Da Nang* → p. 60. The Cham Museum in this modern city is definitely worth a visit. In the 16th century, Spanish and Portuguese sailing ships moored alongside the beach here. They were followed 300 years later by the French navy, and then in March 1965 came the US navy, which transformed this port city into what became the largest American military base in southeast Asia. The legacy of the war lingers on – it could be China Beach, of TV series fame, or the caverns beneath the Marble Mountains, where the Viet Cong had a hideaway. Take a detour to ⑧ *Hai-Van-Pass* → p. 60 between Da Nang and Hue. With a bit of luck, you will be able to enjoy the stunning view over the peninsula and Lang Co lagoon from Cloud Pass at an altitude of 496m (1,625ft).

THE IMPERIAL WORLD

The peaks of the distant Truong Son mountain range rise to a height of 1,400m (4,600ft). In ⑨ *Hue* → p. 69, the city on the Perfume River, you will be immersed into a world of Imperial splendour. In 1802, Emperor Gia Long built his residence and palace here; the tombs of six emperors and the famous ⑩ *Thien Mu Pagoda* → p. 74 draw in travellers from all over the world.

CAVE ADVENTURE AND FAIRY TALE MOUNTAINS

Another fascinating sight awaits you near *Dong Hoi*, where you will find the Unesco-protected ⑪ *Phong Nha Cave* → p. 108. Just as fascinating is the region known as ⑫ *Ha Long Bay on land* → p. 49, which the N 1 crosses near Ninh Binh. It's a fairy-tale landscape dominated by huge green limestone rocks emerging from the rice fields. The teeming capital of ⑬ *Hanoi* → p. 40 is now only approx. 90km (55mi) away.

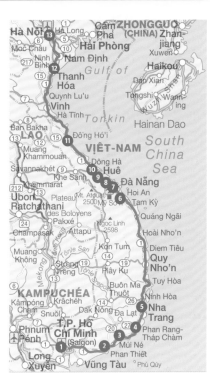

Approx. 1,500km (925mi). Driving time approx. 30 hours, allow 2–3 weeks
Detailed map of the route in the road atlas, the pull-out map and on the back cover

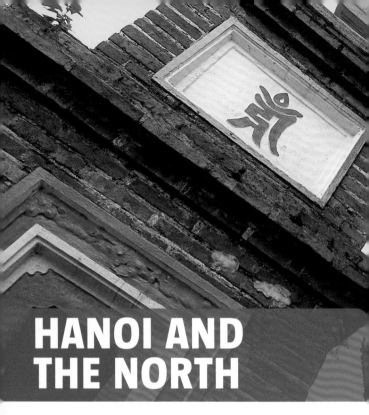

HANOI AND THE NORTH

For a long time Hanoi was regarded as the quieter of the Vietnam's two major cities, but those days are over. A seemingly endless caravan of two-wheelers rattles along the boulevards, past rows of villas, magnificent colonial buildings and the Ho Chi Minh Mausoleum.

There is no holding Hanoi back now; the building boom is even threatening the picturesque artisans' houses in the old quarter. But the enchanting parks, idyllic lakes and the still quiet corners of town more than make up for that.

The north is also full of natural wonders. Southeast of Hanoi, just under two hours away by car, the grey-white limestone rocks of Ha Long Bay jut proudly out of the water. And the mountain village of Sapa is developing rapidly, although it's a long trek by train, if you wish to visit the so-called 'Vietnamese Alps' in the northwest to see the hill tribes and to wander through the cool-temperate rain forest. If you want to visit a tropical rain forest, then include Ba Be National Park, a hidden gem in the north of Vietnam, in your itinerary.

CAO BANG

(133 E1) *(Ⓜ E1)* **Nestling prettily in the mountain landscape, some 700m (2,300ft) above sea level, is the frequently drought-ravaged provincial capital of Cao Bang (pop. 45,000).**
The region near this border town is renowned for its magnificent and wildly overgrown karst hills, free-flowing rivers

Parks, pagodas and new buildings dominate the capital; mountains and the Red River delta the surrounding area

and evergreen rain forests. Perched on a headland between the Bang Giang and Hien rivers stands the town. As a whole day is need to cover the more than 270km (170mi) from Hanoi, the little spot makes a **INSIDER TIPP** good starting point for excursions to Ban Doc and the impressive 53-m (170-ft) high and 300-m (1000-ft) wide *Ban Doc waterfall* (also known as Ban Gioc waterfall), to *Ba Be National Park*, the picturesque *Thang Hen lakes* (four-wheel drive required), *Pac Bo Cave* and the *Narang hill tribe*

market. The town and province is populated mainly by the Tay (Tho), but also by many Nung and some Hmong.

There are a number of good and inexpensive food stalls in the market in *Hoang Nhu*.

MEN QUYEN RESTAURANT

Beside the market is the simple but – clearly among the Vietnamese – the most popular restaurant, as it seems to be nearly always full. You choose your meal directly from the pot. *Tel. 026 3 85 64 33 | Budget*

sizes (satellite TV, telephone, bath tub), partly with a wall view (but quieter than overlooking the street). Tourist information in the lobby, internet. *32 rooms | 159*

Women from the Tay hill tribe carrying heavy loads on bearers

SHOPPING

With a little luck, you can buy finely woven, brightly-coloured carpets made by the Tay and Muong minorities. The carvings here are also of a very high quality. Well worth a visit is the large hill tribe market in *Tra Linh* on the N 3, held on the 4th, 9th, 14th, 19th, 24th and 29th day of the lunar month.

WHERE TO STAY

HUONG THOM HOTEL

A snug hotel with eleven clean rooms – river view from upper floors. The owners (who do not speak English) do their utmost to make guests comfortable. In the street parallel to the market. Sumptuous breakfast. *45 Kim Dong | tel. 026 3 85 58 88 | Budget*

THANH LOAN HOTEL

Located near the Bang Giang river, the hotel boasts simple rooms of varying

Vuon Cam | tel. 026 3 85 70 26 | Budget

INFORMATION

Cao Bang Tourist Information | Phong Lan Hotel | Nguyen Du | tel. 026 3 85 22 45 (if booking excursions, guides and four-wheel drive vehicles, you must call a few days before your arrival)

WHERE TO GO

INSIDER TIPP BA BE NATIONALPARK
(133 D2) (*E2*)

Situated 85km (53mi) southwest of Cao Bang, this region was established as a national park in 1992. It is bordered by mountains over 1,500m (5,000ft) high. This is where the Tay tribe live in their traditional stilt houses. The name Ba Be (Three Bays) indicates that there is water here – namely three interconnected, crystal clear lakes, altogether 8km (5mi) in length, providing the habitat for more than 50 different kinds of freshwater fish. Some 400 plant species thrive in the surrounding tropical rainforest, plus more than 300 animal species, including many monkeys, brightly coloured butterflies and countless birds. A memorable experience here would be to take a boat trip through the nearly 30-m (100-ft) high, approximately 300-m (1000-ft) long *Puong Cave*. It is home not just to countless bats, but the rocks and stalactites look eerie in torchlight.

If you would like to stay near the lakes, then investigate the *Ba Be Hotel (14 bedrooms | tel. 0281 3 87 61 15 | Budget)* in the Tay village of Cho Ra 18km (11mi) away. The accommodation here is perfectly acceptable.

Three-day tours cost around 5,000,000 dong per person (based on two people, e.g. with *Asiatica Travel | www.asiaticatravel.com)*; the price depends on the number of participants and the agency. The cheapest tours are offered in the traveller cafés in Hanoi. A charge of 5,000 dong is payable in the Visitor Center by the park gates. *National park office: tel. 0281 3 89 40 26*

HA LONG BAY

(133 E–F3) (*Ø F3*) ⭐ This spectacular bay is Vietnam's scenic gem. Unsurprisingly, in 1994, it was added to the list of Unesco World Heritage sites.

About 2,000 islands emerge from the waters of the Gulf of Tonkin. The area of the bay corresponds to 580 sq mi, about the size of the Greater London conurbation. There are two possible explanations for its creation. Firstly, a scientific one, which suggests that the rocks were part of the southwestern Chinese limestone plateau, which was flooded by the sea after the last Ice Age. And then a legend: to fend off Mongol invaders, a dragon flew down from the sky and destroyed the landscape with its flailing tail, putting a major ob-

---

⭐ **Ha Long Bay**
Simply outstanding – limestone pinnacles emerging from the sea → p. 35

⭐ **Old Hanoi**
Picturesque artisans' houses and bustling street markets → p. 40

⭐ **Ho Hoan Kiem**
This idyllic city lake in Hanoi is not just a lovers' rendez-vous → p. 43

⭐ **Van Mieu**
Confucian simplicity, but of impressive proportions, the Temple of Literature in Hanoi → p. 43

⭐ **Chua Thay and Chua Tay Phuong**
These two Buddhist pagodas are among Vietnam's crown jewels → p. 48

⭐ **Huong Tich Son**
A magnificent karst landscape and the Chua Huong pilgrims' pagoda → p. 49

⭐ **Ha Long Bay on land**
Impressive karst outcrops near Ninh Binh – rocks as far as the eye can see → p. 49

⭐ **Sapa**
Get close to the colourfully-dressed hill tribes in the rugged mountains of the northwest → p. 50

MARCO POLO HIGHLIGHTS

stacle in front of the approaching cavalry. The dragon then dived into the sea, so the water would flood the valley.

What used to be the two separate fishing ports of *Hon Gai* and *Bai Chay* are now called *Ha Long City* and are connected by a bridge. They have merged to become one large and lively playground – with an uninterrupted and expanding skyline of hotels, a night market, a casino, an overpriced water puppet theatre and a giant circus arena on the *Tuan Chau peninsula* 5km (3mi) away.

LOW BUDGET

▶ ● What does the future hold? Fortune tellers among the hill tribe minorities in Cao Bang or Sapa will tell you your fate, for only 30,000 dong. A village shaman will perform fireside rituals using stones and bamboo poles as a 'phone' to contact ancestors and spirits.

▶ Everything is just right at the Sunset Hotel opposite the pier – great, clean rooms (satellite TV, air conditioning) with harbour view and friendly, helpful hosts (Mr Tung and his wife). They will also keep you up-to-date with all the inside information. *Cat Ba | Promenade (1/4 Street no. 180) | tel. 031 3 88 83 70 | approx. 300,000 dong*

▶ It's even cheaper on Cat Ba – you can camp on the beach at *Cat Co 2* and on *Monkey Island (approx. 100,000 to 300,000 dong per tent, mattress and lighting included, but you will have to bring most of your own food).*

SIGHTSEEING

CAVES
The attraction of Ha Long Bay lies primarily in the countless dripstone caves that can be explored as part of a boat tour.

The *Hang Dau Go* or the Cave of Wooden Stakes is so named, because during the 13th century it was used as a hiding place for a large collection of sharp bamboo poles, which the northern Vietnamese people used to put 500,000 Mongols under Kublai Khan to flight. The cave is reached via 90 steps.

Do try to visit the *Hang Trong,* the Drum Cave. Wind and weather cause the stalagmites and stalactites to emit noises, said to resemble distant drumbeats.

The finest cave of all is the strikingly illuminated *Hang Sung Sot.* The tour groups are dispersed around the three vast chambers; this way they can enjoy the circular tour with its almost mystical vistas in relative peace.

Boat tours around the bay start in Bai Chay or from Cat Ba island.

FOOD & DRINK

INSIDER TIPP **KIM HANG RESTAURANT**
Five floors dedicated to feasting – among the specialities of this fish restaurant, which is very popular with coach parties, are the seafood menus with crabs, fish fillets, prawns and squid. *123 Ha Long Rd | Bai Chay | approx. 4km (3mi) from the town centre towards Tuan Chau | 033 3 84 68 09 | www.nhahangkimhang.com | Moderate–Expensive*

PHUONG OANH RESTAURANT
Small family restaurant, lots of seafood on the menu. Breakfasts also served. *Ha Long Rd on the corner opposite the post office and the Thong Nhat Hotel | Bai Chay | tel. 033 3 84 61 45 | Budget*

SHOPPING

NIGHT MARKET IN BAI CHAY

There's something going on here every night – piled high on the tables between the promenade and beach are chopsticks, swimwear, shoes, toys and knick-knacks of all kinds. And there's a small funfair for children. *Daily 6pm–11pm*

SPORTS & ACTIVITIES

BOAT TOURS

For trips out on to Ha Long Bay and to Cat Ba island, go to the tourist pier in Bai Chay (near the Thang Long Hotel) for tickets and boats *(from approx. 700,000 dong/per boat per day, depending on group size and type of boat)*. Waiting for passengers to arrive are some 300 or so boats, junks and paddle steamers. Ha Long tours also leave from Cat Ba. Because now all boats (up to 50!) can anchor in one bay, be prepared for plenty of diesel fumes and karaoke-style speaker systems.

KAYAKING

If you want to do more than just potter around the bay, you can explore some of the caves by taking a kayak through a narrow opening and then paddling into the emerald green lagoon (e.g. into the *Hang Luon Cave*). Or you can make a detour to the 'floating' fishing villages, such as *Van Gia,* where even the school floats on the water.

ENTERTAINMENT

TRUNG NGUYEN 2

It's impossible to overlook or ignore this bar. A popular place to chat over fruit juices, beer, whisky, ice cream, iced coffee and snacks. *Ha Long Road (Promenade) | Bai Chay | tel. 033 3 84 43 38 | Budget*

WHERE TO STAY

ATLANTIC HOTEL ⚘

A hotel in bauhaus style with an airy, terraced restaurant. Rooms furnished in a modern style on five floors (satellite

Light show in Hang Sung Sot Cave

TV, telephone, some with balcony). *52 rooms | Tuan Chau | tel. 033 3 84 28 42 | www.atlantichotel.com.vn | Moderate*

HERITAGE HOTEL

Small rooms, some with rocking chairs, marble baths and balcony. Suite with heating and fireplace. Also part of the hotel – a quiet pool and a loud karaoke disco. *101 rooms | 88 Ha Long Rd. (Prom-*

INSIDER TIPP ▶ **VIETHOUSE LODGE** ☼ ☺
Rustic-style rooms with old roof beams, swing doors, lots of rattan, terracotta and wood, satellite TV, terraced restaurant, pool, sauna, tours, internet. Guests stay in rooms built in traditional nha san architectural style, timber houses where many of the ethnic minorities live. *28 rooms | Tuan Chau | tel. 033 3 84 22 07 | www.viethouselodge.com | Moderate*

A floating fishing village in Ha Long Bay

enade) *| Bai Chay | tel. 033 3 84 68 88 | www.heritagehalonghotel.com | Moderate–Expensive*

HOLIDAY VILLA HALONG BAY (AU LAC RESORT) ☼

The villas and rooms, some perhaps in need of renovation, are situated by a private beach or by a hill (large baths, some with jacuzzi) with an amazing panoramic view. Pool, massages, fitness suite, golf course, helicopter flights over the bay. *247 rooms | Tuan Chau | tel. 033 3 84 29 99 | www.holidayvillahalongbay.com | Moderate–Expensive*

INFORMATION

Tourist Service Center | Bai Chay Pier | Ha Long City | tel. 033 3 84 41 90 and 3 84 74 81 | www.halongbay.com.vn

WHERE TO GO

BAI TU LONG BAY (133 F3) *(ω F–G3)*
This northern bay is much quieter than Ha Long Bay. There are not so many spectacular caves, but instead you will find several largish beaches, such as on the islands of *Quan Lan* and *Van Don*. King prawns and fish are farmed on Quan Lan and you can still witness some of the surviving traditions, such

the boat races that form part of the village festival in the summer. But as you walk the streets and explore the main village, you will see men at work sawing and hammering. Once the first bungalows are finished, there are bound to be more – on both islands' beaches. Several ferries per day ply between Cam Pha on the mainland and Quan Lan; they also leave from Hon Gai (Ha Long City). You will find a number of places to stay on the island, e.g. the INSIDER TIPP *Min Chau Beach Resort*, a small modern and professionally-run three star hotel near the beach with decent rooms and suites (if a little overpriced), mini-pool, roof bar *(50 rooms | Minh Chau Beach | tel. 033 3 99 50 16 | mobile 090 4 08 18 68 | www. minhchauresort.com | Moderate).*

If all you need is a bed for the night, you could try the *Robinson (Budget),* but the cabins are rather spartan. Better, inexpensive accommodation with air-conditioning and hot showers is to be found in the town, e.g. the new, four-storey *Ann Hotel* with 26 nice balcony rooms and large modern bathrooms *(tel. 033 3 87 78 89 | mobile 0913 07 20 72 | www.ann hotel.com.vn | Budget).*

The island of *Van Don* further north is connected to the mainland by a bridge. There are two ferries a day from Quan Lan or you can catch the hydrofoil from Ha Long City. At *Bai Dai beach* at the eastern end of Van Don, it's still quite rural, but it's changing fast. You can't miss all the new building work taking place along this part of the coast. An endless stream of freighters, boats and ferries ply across the bay against the magnificent backdrop of rocky islets. Van Don was in fact the first commercial fishing port in the Ly dynasty – and that was over 1,000 years ago. A very affordable place to spend the night is the INSIDER TIPP *Bai Tu Long Eco Resort (Bai Dai | tel. 033 3*

79 31 56 | tel. in Hanoi 04 37 84 94 00 | Budget) – 50 simple rooms in rows of villas on stilts (air-conditioning, parquet floors). The beach is only 100m away.

CAT BA (133 E3) (*∅ F3*)

Cat Ba is the largest island in Ha Long Bay and lies some 20km (12mi) southwest of Ha Long City. In the main town, *Cat Ba*, mini-hotels abound, as at weekends it is the preferred destination for countless trippers, mainly young people, seeking the pleasures of the karaoke bars. However, since 1986 a large part of the island has been designated as a conservation area, so there are limits on how far the tourist developments can go. Wooded slopes extending to a height of 300m (1,000ft), deep gorges, caves and grottoes, as well as beaches enclosed by rocks form a small, Polynesian-style area, a perfect habitat for monkeys and bird species. The best time of year for swimming in the sea is from June to October, at other times it is often cool and misty. If you join a tour of Cat Ba National Park, you can visit caves, where stone implements and human bones thought to be up to 7,000 years old were found (admission approx. 40,000 dong).

Tapas and pasta, soups and salads, vegetarian fare and seafood served in the *Green Mango (near the Holiday View Hotel | tel. 031 3 88 71 51 | Moderate).* Chic ambience by the promenade. Alternatively try *The Good Bar 8 (1/4 Street No. 4 (Promenade) | tel. 031 3 68 84 50 | Budget)* where climbers meet to discuss their conquests over pizzas, hamburgers and Vietnamese dishes, plus pool, table football and darts.

Beside a small bay lies the villa-style beach hotel *Sunrise Resort (39 rooms | Cat Co 3 beach | tel. 031 3 88 73 60 | www.catbasunriseresort.com | Moderate–Expensive)* with nice rooms (some with jacuzzi), pool, three restaurants and water sports. The ✳ *Holiday View Hotel (120 rooms | Road 1/4, at the eastern end of the promenade | tel. 031 3 88 72 00 | www.holidayviewhotel-catba.com | Moderate)* is a good, if slightly tired, 14-storey hotel with balcony rooms and panorama bar. Cat Ong (approx. 5km/3mi southeast of Cat Ba) is only a small, jungle island, but decent accommodation is available in the *Ocean Beach Resort (14 rooms | tel. 031 2 62 49 19 | Reservations: Ocean Tours Hanoi, tel. 04 39 26 04 63 | www.oceanbeachresort.com.vn | Moderate)*. Seven rather basic palm-leaf-roofed twin huts (no sound-proofing!) by the beach or on the hill; beach barbecue, kayak tours.

HAI PHONG (133 E3) (*∅ F3*)

At first glance the atmosphere in Vietnam's third largest city (pop. 700,000), just over 100km (65mi) southeast of Hanoi on the Song Cam river, is hard to identify. But very quickly the colonial past of Hai Phong, which was expanded in 1876 by the French into a port, becomes evident. Explore the *Quartier français* around Dien Bien Phu and you will find villas, small mansions, hotels and colonnades.

Adjoining to the east is the Old Town. The pretty, 18th-century *Den Nghe* temple *(corner of Le Chan/Me Linh)* is dominated by a richly ornamented stone altar.

The welcoming *Saigon Café (107 Dien Bien Phu | tel. 031 3 82 21 95 | Budget)* is now a meeting place for travellers from all over the world; often Western-style live music in the evenings. The elegant, colonial-style *Harbour View Hotel (127 rooms | 4 Tran Phu | tel. 031 3 82 78 27 | www.harbourviewvietnam.com | Moderate–Expensive)* is highly recommended. Many coach trips are organised here. The *Huu Nghi Hotel (172 rooms | 60 Dien Bien Phu | tel. 031 3 82 32 44 | www.huunghi*

hotel.vn | Moderate) is an elegant city hotel with pool and bar (10th floor).

Several times a day ferries leave from *Ben Binh terminal* to Cat Ba island (slow boat 2 hrs, hydrofoil approx. 30 minutes). *Information: Vietnam Tourism | 60 A Dien Bien Phu | tel. 031 3 84 29 57*

HANOI

MAP ON PAGE 138–139

(133 D3) (*∅ E3*) The city of Hanoi (pop. approx. 2.5–3 million) stands proudly at the heart of a fertile plain 139km (86mi) above the mouth of the Red River (Song Hong) in the Gulf of Tonkin.

Spacious parks and about 600 temples, pagodas and magnificent buildings from the European colonial era shape the face of this city, which was founded in 1010, but not named *Ha Noi* or the 'city on the bend of the river' until the days of Emperor Minh Mang (1820–41). Only after the economic boom reached in the north of Vietnam did this vast metropolis finally get moving. Mopeds roar through the streets, the noise of construction work is ever-present, housing and office blocks are springing up everywhere, and evidence of the city's commercial revival is to be seen in the emergence of several luxury hotels.

SIGHTSEEING

OLD HANOI ★ (138–139 C–D 2–3)

No visitor could possibly ignore Hanoi's Old Quarter. The artisans' district, which was first settled in the 11th century, when Emperor Ly Thai To moved the capital to Thang Long, is a fascinating sight. Arranged around the Imperial Palace was a ring of 36 villages, each one represent-

CITY **WHERE TO START?**
Start your tour of the city with a walk round **Lake Hoan Kiem (139 D3–4)** on the edge of Hanoi's Old Quarter – from the French (hotel) quarter at the southern end of the lake and then on past the 'gymnasts' (early morning and evening), passing the Jade Mountain Temple and then on into the heart of Old Quarter. If you're a long way from the starting point, take a moped taxi. Or you could catch a bus there, nos. 1, 3, 7 or 14 *(www.hanoibus.com)*.

ing a different craft or trade. Guilds and trading associations were formed. The '36 streets' from that time have survived the centuries. Each street is named after the goods that were once made and sold there. *So Hang Ca* is Fish Lane, *Hang Bo* Basket Street, *Hang Buom* Sailmakers' Alley, *Hang Non* for hatters and *Hang Hom* for the carpenters, who made cof-

fins. Unfortunately, the brick houses from the 19th century are threatened by the current construction boom. Even the shop displays have adapted to meet the requirements of the throngs of tourists. From 3pm, but at its height from 5pm to 9pm, amid the fumes two-wheel chaos reigns in the Old Quarter. Bustling throngs block the way, it's sometimes almost impossible to move, either because the narrow pavements are overflowing with parked mopeds or the hopelessly congested streets are crammed with hundreds of 'Tigers' revving loudly and constantly hooting. If there's room, they simply ride on the pavement – often at breakneck speed. The best solution is to simply make light of it all, so just find an unoccupied spot and watch and wait, or disappear into one of the smart cafés for a tea or find an air-conditioned bar for a *bia hoi* beer...

CHUA MOT COT (138 A2)
There's a charming legend behind the One Pillar Pagoda. One night the goddess Quan Am appeared before the age-

A colourful backdrop – noisy mopeds in Hanoi's Old Quarter

ing and childless emperor, Ly Thai To, and presented him with a baby boy. There was now a male heir in the royal family and so, out of gratitude to the goddess,

The Huc bridge crosses to the Ngoc Son Temple

Ly Thai To built a stone pillar as a memorial shrine in the form of a lotus flower. In 1954 the column was destroyed by the French, but a concrete replica was built as a replacement. Quan Am is still revered as a symbol of fertility. *Daily sunrise to sunset | on Chua Mot Cot street, south of the Ho Chi Minh Mausoleum*

CHUA QUAN SU (138 C4)

The Ambassadors' Pagoda is always a hive of activity, but then it is the city's Buddhist centre. During the 15th century

the building was used as a hostel for emissaries from other countries. *Daily approx. 6am–9pm | 73 Quan Su*

DEN NGOC SON (139 D3)

The Jade Mountain Temple, which stands on an island in the northern Lake Hoan Kiem is dedicated to three individuals: General Tran Hung Dao, who defeated the Mongols during the 13th century, the scholar Van Xuong, and La Tho, the patron saint of physicians. You can reach the temple via the pretty The Huc bridge (Bridge of the Rising Sun). *Daily 8am–5pm | admission 10,000 dong*

DEN TRAN VU (138 B1)

The Den Tran Vu Temple, the most important Taoist temple in Hanoi, was built in 1010 outside the city gates. It is dedicated to the demon and sorcerer, Huyen Thien Tran Vu. His statue was placed outside the central zone; his job to protect the capital from malevolent spirits. The 4-m (13-ft) high bronze version of Tran Vu, weighing nearly 4 tonnes, dates from 1677. *Daily 8am–6pm | Quan Thanh, on the southeastern shore of the West Lake | admission 5,000 dong*

INSIDER TIPP MUSEUM OF ETHNOLOGY ● (0)

Beautifully-presented exhibitions on the culture, settlement patterns, implements, costumes, crafts and minority religions of Vietnam, with many replica buildings outside. *Tue–Sun 8.30am–5.30pm | Nguyen Van Huyen, on the northern outskirts on the route to the airport | no.14 bus from Bo Ho (car park on the north bank of Lake Hoan Kiem) as far as the Hoang Quoc Viet arterial road, alighting at the Nghia Tan stop, then 5 minutes on foot (signposted), total journey time 25 minutes | www.vme.org.vn | admission 25,000 dong*

HO CHI MINH HOUSE (138 A2)

Long queues regularly form outside the wooden house, where Ho Chi Minh lived from 1958 until his death in 1969. So any insights into the life of Bac Ho (or Uncle Ho) from the rather sparse office, the no less spartan bedroom and the pond, where he often sat and mused, can be time limited. *Daily 8am–11am, 1.30pm–4pm | Ba Dinh Square, next to the Presidential Palace (in the park) | admission 10,000 dong*

HO CHI MINH MAUSOLEUM (138 A2)

Built between 1973 and 1975, the massive blocks of red, black and grey marble create an awe-inspiring memorial for the last resting place of Ho Chi Minh's embalmed body. In silence and usually in a long queue, visitors parade past the glass coffin containing the mortal remains of the country's great revolutionary hero. It was here on the square in front of the mausoleum, where on 2 September 1945, Ho Chi Minh declared Vietnam's independence. ● With full military pomp, a flag is hoisted every morning at 6am and then lowered again at 9pm. *April–Sept Tue–Thu 7.30am–10.30am, Sat, Sun 7.30am–11am, Dec–Mar, Tue–Thu 8–11, Sat, Sun 8am–11.30am (Oct/Nov closed for 1 month) | Ba Dinh Square | ● admission free | no admission in shorts, miniskirts and tank tops | cameras to be handed in*

HO CHI MINH MUSEUM (138 A3)

Russian and Vietnamese artists worked together to design the exhibitions. The section entitled 'Past' uses an eclectic mix of memorabilia, including photographs and documents, to celebrate more than just the life and achievements of Ho Chi Minh. Assembled on the second floor, under the title 'Future', is a collection of revolutionary art and other symbolic ar-

tefacts. The museum was opened in 1990 to mark Ho Chi Minh's 100th birthday. *Tue–Sun 8am–noon, 1.30pm–4.30pm | Ngoc Ha | admission 10,000 dong*

HO HOAN KIEM ★ (139 D3–4)

Legend has it that in the 15th century at the Lake of the Returned Sword the heroic Le Loi took a powerful sword from a golden turtle in the lake and used it to drive the Chinese out of Vietnam. Having successfully banished the occupying army, the magic sword was seized from Le Loi's sheath by the turtle and restored to the lake. As a gesture of gratitude, the *Thap Rua* or Turtle Tower, was built on an island in the middle of the lake. ● Every morning between 5am and 7pm, the lakeside resembles a fitness centre, as joggers, gymnasts, plus tai chi and aerobic enthusiasts meet to get their daily fix of exercise. It costs nothing to join in.

INSIDER TIPP ▶ 'TUBE HOUSE' IN MA MAY STREET (139 D3)

This wooden house dating from the 19th century is in fine shape. It was restored in the late 1990s and then opened to visitors. It is a typical example of this kind of very narrow building, known as a 'tube house'. Put on the carpet slippers and you will be amazed. Have a look, for example, at the finely carved swing doors, the brick carvings, which promise a long life, and on the upper floor the beautiful antique bed with mother-of-pearl decorations. *Daily 8am–5pm | 87 Ma May | admission 5,000 dong*

VAN MIEU ★ ● (138 B4)

Ly Thanh Tong, the third ruler of the Ly Dynasty, had this Temple of Literature built in 1070 in honour of Confucius. Only six years later, his successor, Ly Nhan Tong founded Vietnam's first university in an adjoining property: Quoc Tu Giam, the Institute for Sons of the State. The 70m by 350m Van Mieu complex consists of a strict sequence of gates and courtyards, with the shrine of Confucius on the northern side. There are four gates to pass through, symbolising the tests that are needed to achieve Heavenly Clarity. The path begins at Quoc Tu Giam street, thereafter it passes through the *Van Mieu Portal* in the forecourt. The paved path leads up to the *Dai Trung* gate, the Gate of the Great Middle, and then to the *Khue Van Cac* gate: the Pleiades Gate, a pavilion dating from 1805, named after the constellation considered to be important for scholars. Literary debates and poetry readings were held here. In the courtyard at the rear, stone turtles, symbols of wisdom, are clustered around the *Thien Quang Tinh,* the Well of Heavenly Clarity. They bear 82 stone stelae, dating from between 1442 and 1779, inscribed with the names of the Confucian Academy's successful graduates.

Pass through the *Dai Thanh* Gate (Gate of Great Success) and enter the fourth most important courtyard in the temple buildings and the ceremonial hall honouring Confucius' 76 wisest disciples. Behind it is the fifth and final court, *Thai Hoc*, where you will find a museum, on the second floor of which are altars with statues of the three kings, Ly Nhan Tong, Ly Thanh Tong and Le Thanh Tong. *Daily 8am–5pm | admission 5,000 dong*

CITADEL (138 B–C 2–3)

For over 50 years it was a closed off as a military zone, but the first rebuilt sections are now open to the public. Completed between 1802 and 1812, it was built on the orders of Emperor Gia Long to a design drawn up by French military architects. In 2010 it became a Unesco World Heritage Site. Given the fact that French possessed the original plans, it was not difficult for them in 1872 to capture the stronghold and destroy most of it. Visi-

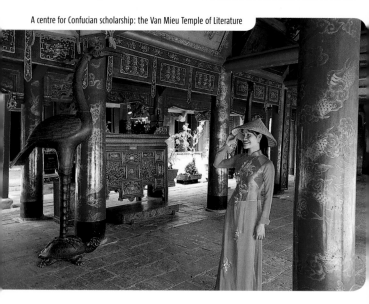

A centre for Confucian scholarship: the Van Mieu Temple of Literature

tors can enter the inner citadel via the northern *Cua Bac* gate, the west gate in Phung Hung street or the *Doan Mon* central gate at the level of the Ho Chi Minh Mausoleum. *Wed–Sun 8am–11.30am, 1.30pm–5pm | admission 25,000 dong*

FOOD & DRINK

There are a number of good food stalls on the western edge of Old Quarter in *Tong Duy Tan* and *Cam Chi*, about 500m northeast of the station. Outside the Old Quarter, there are many food and pho soup stalls, in *Le Van Huu* (139 D–E5), for example.

LE BON CAFÉ (139 E4)

A beautiful garden restaurant with a large interior serves international cuisine, a breakfast buffet and also barbecue food. The waiting staff are professional, friendly and work at a brisk pace. Wine only by the bottle. Also, live music from 9pm. *1 Pham Ngu Lao | tel. 04 39 33 58 11 | Moderate*

DAC KIM (138 C3)

One of Hanoi's top food stands – try the *bun cha* (pork meatballs with rice noodles) and the delicious nem (spring rolls). *1 Hang Manh | tel. 04 38 28 50 22 | Budget*

FOODSHOP 45 (138 B1)

Well away from all the traffic, the idyllic Lake Truc Bach is – INSIDER TIPP the perfect place to take a quiet stroll... and then sample the best Indian food in north Vietnam courtesy of the two brothers, Cuong and Hue. Relaxed atmosphere near Sunset View. *59 Truc Bach near the West Lake | tel. 04 37 16 29 59 | Budget*

INSIDER TIPP HIGHWAY 4 (139 D3)

Café bar with the best self-distilled brandies in the whole of Vietnam. Marvellous north Vietnamese cuisine, including specialities from the hill tribes. Cookery courses. *5 Hang Tre | tel. 04 39 26 06 39 | and 54 May Hac De (139 D6) and 575 Kim Ma (0) | www.highway4.com | Moderate*

INDOCHINE (138 B4)

Award-winning Vietnamese cuisine at its finest in elegant surroundings with traditional musical accompaniment. Popular with coach parties at lunchtime. *16 Nam Ngu | tel. 04 39 42 40 97 | Expensive*

SAWADEE (138 C4)

Great little Thai restaurant serving delicacies from Vietnam's neighbour. Dining on two floors, at the higher level on a small veranda. *52A Ly Thuong Kiet | tel. 04 39 34 55 89 | Budget*

LA VERTICALE (139 D5)

Five-star chef Didier Corlou conjures up some highly desirable creations. *Sun closed for lunch | 19 Ngo Van So | tel. 04 39 44 63 17 | www.verticale-hanoi.com | Expensive*

SHOPPING

Hang Gai, Hang Bong and Hang Trong are streets in the Old Quarter with many tailors and shops selling silk products. Hang Gai and Hang Bom also specialise in galleries and crafts, around St Joseph's Cathedral. In Na Tho and Hang Trong you'll find some rather expensive boutiques, while Luong Van Can is the place for bespoke ao dais. That's not forgetting Hang Bac (silverware, jewellery, propaganda posters and crafts from the hill tribes), Lan Ong (herbal 'medicinal' remedies, e.g. snake brandy) and Hang Buom (sweets).

LA BOUTIQUE (138 C4)

La Boutique sells high quality, sometimes highly original painted silk fabrics and other fashionable garments made from silk. *6 Na Tho | near St Joseph's Cathedral*

Todeco | 91 A/5 Ly Nam De | (138 C2–3) *| tel. 04 38 23 57 67 | tel. 04 37 47 23 33 | www.todeco-vn.com.* Customised tours, English-speaking tour guides.

Red is the colour of happiness – a snapshot of Hang Da market

CRAFT LINK AND HOA SEN GALLERY (138 B4)

Crafts (especially woven fabrics from the tribal hills) and some beautiful souvenirs. The proceeds go to projects supporting minorities and Hanoi street children. *43 and 51 Van Mieu | near the Temple of Literature | www.craftlink.com.vn*

MARKET (138 C2)

● The huge *Dong Xuan market* with market hall sells hats, fruit, vegetables, karaoke systems (!) and much more – until midnight.

SPORTS & ACTIVITIES

Ocean Tours | 22 Hang Bac | (139 D3) *| tel. 04 39 26 04 63 | www.oceantours.com.vn* A reliable operator for tours of the north.

INSIDER TIP ▶ **KING'S ISLAND GOLF RESORT & COUNTRY CLUB** (133 D3) *(ｱ E3)*

36-hole course about 35km (22mi) west of the crystal-clear Dong Mo reservoir at the foot of the Mount Ba Vi. The *Dong Mo* hotel *(Son Tay Village | tel. 04 33 68 65 55 | www.kingsislandgolf.com | Expensive)* offers exclusive accommodation.

ENTERTAINMENT

JAZZCLUB MINH'S (138 C4)

Bar owner Minh teaches saxophone at the Hanoi Conservatory, so you can expect some high-class live jazz here *(daily from 9pm).* Daily from 10am *| 65 Quan Su | south of the Hoan Kiem district | tel. 04 39 42 04 00 | www.minhjazzvietnam.com*

LATINO CLUB (138 C4)
Disco in the Melía Hotel with salsa or merengue performed by live Latin American bands. *44 B Ly Thuong Kiet | tel. 04 39 34 33 43*

OPERA HOUSE (139 E4)
Programme includes classical concerts, theatre performances (often in Vietnamese) and dance. For up-to-date listings, see, for example, Vietnam News. *Nha Hat Lon | 1 Trang Tien | tel. opera house 04 38 25 43 12 | tel. theatre 04 39 33 01 31 | tickets from 75,000 dong*

PHUC TAN BAR (139 D2)
Hip club with international DJs. If you don't want to dance, you can play pool, table football or just chill out on the sofas on the awesome Sunset Terrace with view over the Red River *(until 4am)*. *51 Phuc Tan*

INSIDER TIPP ▶ WATER PUPPET THEATRE (139 D3)
Eleven actors operate the puppets to music played by wooden flutes, gongs, drums and the dan bau, the single-string box zither. It doesn't matter if you don't understand the Vietnamese, it's easy to follow the action. You can see the fisherman struggling with his prey, you hear the rice growing, watch a jaguar hunt and encounter fire-breathing dragons. Performances usually last for over an hour. *Thang Long Water Puppet Theatre | daily 4pm, 6pm and 8pm, subject to demand also approx. 5pm and 9pm | 57 Dinh Tien Doang | tel. 04 39 36 43 35 | www.thanglongwaterpuppet.org | admission 50,000 to 90,000 dong (buy your ticket well in advance) | also at Hanoi Water Park (614 Lac Long Can, West Lake)* (0)

WHERE TO STAY

INSIDER TIPP ▶ GREEN MANGO (138 C3)
Fashionable boutique hotel in the Old Quarter. You are sure to get a warm welcome from the Nguyens. Five floors (no lift) in stylishly furnished rooms with parquet flooring, large modern bathrooms (jacuzzi in the *Sweet*) and fresh fruit. Book in advance! The hotel's restaurant is one of the best in the Old Quarter – creative Asian-style nouvelle cuisine *(Expensive)*. *15 rooms | 18 Hang Quat | tel. 04 39 28 99 16 | www.greenmango.vn | Moderate*

INSIDER TIPP ▶ HANOI BOUTIQUE HOTEL 1 (138–139 C–D2)
Modern, parquet-floor rooms and suites with flat screen TV, some rather small in plush 1950s style. Room 704 on the 7th floor is a lovely, quiet deluxe room with view. French/Vietnamese restaurant and bar. *56 rooms | 7 Ngo Gach | Hoan Kiem district | tel. 04 39 33 22 88 | www.hanoi boutiquehotel.vn | Moderate–Expensive*

HANOI SERENITY HOTEL (138 C3)
Relatively new, but smallish hotel with smart rooms and high comfort level at a low price (satellite TV, minibar, breakfast included), professional team, always willing to help, central location. *17 rooms | 1 B Cua Dong (west of the Old Quarter) | tel. 04 39 23 35 49 | www.hanoiserenityhotel.com | Budget–Moderate*

HONG NGOC (138 C4)
Hostel in a popular mini-chain, with large, well-equipped rooms (some with safe, balcony), near Lake Hoan Kiem. Tours of surrounding area can be booked in the hotel. *50 rooms | 34 Hang Manh and 39 | Hang Bac | tel. 04 38 28 50 53 | www.hongngochotel.com | Moderate*

LUCKY 2 HOTEL (138 C3)
Rooms furnished in Vietnamese style with satellite TV and telephone. There's another Lucky Hotel in *Hang Trong no. 12 | 22 rooms | 46 Hang Hom | tel. 04 3 92 81 70 | luckyhotel.com.vn | Moderate*

MELÍA HANOI ✈ (138 C4)
Centrally located multi-storey hotel belonging to the luxury Spanish chain. Huge lobby, with pool, sauna, tennis, salsa club and helicopter landing pad. *306 rooms | 44 B Ly Thuong Kiet | tel. 04 39 34 33 43 | tel. in UK 0808 234 17 | www.meliahanoi.solmelia.com | Moderate–Expensive*

SOFITEL LEGEND METROPOLE (139 D4)
The best hotel in town. Stay in the renovated old wing and bask in the opulence of the colonial era. The *Opera Wing*, opened in 1996, may be more luxurious, but less atmospheric. The ● chocolate buffet in the afternoon is stupendous. *244 rooms | 15 Ngo Quyen | tel. 04 38 26 69 19 | www.sofitel.com | Expensive*

INFORMATION

TIC (Tourist Information Center) | 7 Dinh Tien Hoang | near Lake Hoa Kiem | (139 D3) | tel. 04 39 26 33 66

WHERE TO GO

CHUA THAY AND CHUA TAY PHUONG
★ (133 D3) (*⌀ E3*)
Situated in the heart of a fertile, rice-growing area, approx. 40km (25mi) west of Hanoi, only a few kilometres apart, are these two magnificent pagodas *(admission to both 15,000 dong)*.
The ✈ Tay Phuong Pagoda near the village of Thach Xa stands on a hillock 50m (160ft) in height. To reach it, you will have to climb around 260 steps, but it is worth the effort, if only for the fine view and a close look at the three iron-wood buildings with elegant upward-sweeping eaves, beautifully adorned with dragons, unicorns, phoenix and turtles. Visitors also get to admire the precious statues of the 18 la han or the 'enlightened ones': 62 filigree figures, masterfully carved from the hard wood of the jack fruit tree.
Situated by Lake Long Tri near the village of Sai Son at the foot of a limestone peak and surrounded by temples and pavilions is Chua Thay or the Master's Pagoda. It is dedicated to the miracle-worker and sorcerer, Tu Dao, who withdrew to the mountain in the 12th century to meditate and to disseminate the teachings of the Buddha. Tu Dao is also the patron saint of water puppeteers.

CUC PHUONG NATIONAL PARK ☺
(133 D4) (*⌀ E3*)
Cuc Phuong is Vietnam's largest national park. Situated some 135km (85mi) southwest of Hanoi, the mainly tropical forest covers an area of 223sq km (86sq mi). As well as some giant 1,000-year-old trees, it is also home to squirrels, countless butterflies, approx. 320 different bird species, 120 reptile species and a very varied range of flora. The rocky outcrops rise to a height of 600m (2,000ft). No fewer than ten trekking trails criss-cross this unique primeval forest. In 1987 the Delacour's langur, originally thought to be extinct, was rediscovered here. This long-tailed, tree-dwelling monkey is just one of several animal species in a small *monkey sanctuary (Endangered Primate Rescue Center | daily 9am–11am and 1.30pm–4pm | www.primatecenter.org)*. Facilities, including hotels, villas, a camp-site and restaurants (usually full at the weekend),

have been developed to attract more visitors to the park. October to December and March/April are the best months for a visit. *Tel. 030 3 84 80 06 | www.cucphuongtourism.com | admission (with*

advised to hire a guide (charge approx. 300,000 dong).

Under the ⭐ *Huong Tich Son* (Mountain of Fragrant Vestiges), located deep inside magnificent karst countryside, lie

A Delacour's langur welcomes visitors to Cuc Phuong National Park

guide for the Primate Center) approx. 30,000 dong

HOA BINH AND HUONG TICH SON
(133 D3–4) (*E3*)

There would be no reason for any tourist to visit the non-descript provincial capital of Hoa Binh (close to the banks of the Song Da and the Ho Song Da reservoir), approx. 75km (45mi) southwest of Hanoi, were it not so near to one of Vietnam's most important places of pilgrimage, the *Perfume Pagoda (Chua Huong)*. Most of the visitors are locals, who come to these parts to explore the Muong hill tribe's villages, such as *Ban Dam* or *Giang,* and to admire the impressive, stilted longhouses. The *Mai Chau valley* is home to a number of minorities, including the Black and mainly White Thai. If you would like a conducted tour, you are

the *Huong Tich cave* and the famous Perfume Pagoda. To reach this chua, built in honour of the Goddess of Mercy, Quan Am, you have to take a boat trip (many people make this tour as a day trip from Hanoi, approx. 300,000 dong). Thousands of pilgrims make their way to the temples and shrines for the New Year festivals, but also in March and April and at weekends. A modern cable car takes visitors up to the pagoda complex grotto on the mountain. Alternatively, you can make the strenuous, approx. two-hour climb (sturdy shoes essential).

HA LONG BAY ON LAND ⭐
(133 D4) (*E4*)

Rising abruptly and seemingly without any base from a sea of dark green are wooded cones, rocky tips and mountain ridges. So it's no surprise that this bizarre karst landscape, some 90km (56mi) south of Hanoi has quickly become a top tourist attraction. The limestone formations, which have emerged over millennia, are comparable in beauty with Ha Long Bay – the difference being, there's no sea, only a river. In the heart of this spectacular landscape lies the provincial capital of *Ninh Binh.* Despite a population of around 53,000, the town was formerly not much more than a pretty village. But that changed when independent travellers discovered the region. The most popular spot is the town of *Tam Coc* (10km/6mi west of Ninh Binh), where the boats for the tours along the river are moored. For large, well-equipped (multibed) rooms and a huge restaurant, try the *Anh Dzung Hotel (13 rooms | Tam Coc, opposite the booking office | tel. 030 3 61 80 20 | anhdzung_tamcoc@yahoo.com | Budget). The Long Hotel (10 rooms | Tam Coc | tel. 030 3 61 80 77 | www.hotelninh binh.com | Budget)* boasts a ⊰⊱ terrace and a large restaurant. *Information is in the hotels and on arrival in Tam Coc (admission, incl. boat 70,000 dong)*

SAPA

(132 B2) (*ᗉ C2*) ★ **Sapa was developed by the French about 100 years ago as a spa and military sanatorium. Pretty villas, fortress-like country houses and a church recall the colonial era.**

Although Sapa (pop. 38,000) is a remote spot and the coldest and mistiest place in Vietnam (best time to visit: September to November), it has become a bustling tourist destination, in fact at the weekends, it's so crowded you can hardly move.

The little town is spread across hilly terrain at a height of 1,550m (5,000ft) at the foot of the Fan Si Pan (Phan Si Pang), a mountain often shrouded by low cloud, the Alpine Hoang Lien Son range forming the backdrop. The main attractions here are mainly the magnificent mountain scenery and the hill tribes with their colourful costumes. Among the long-standing traditions of the hill tribes are the construction of stilt houses, a belief in natural spirits, betel nut chewing, tooth blackening and eyebrow shaving.

The usual way to reach the town is via Lao Cai (37km/23mi northeast of Sapa), but there is an alternative. In 1922 a railway line was laid between Hanoi and Lao Cai, but only guests of the Victoria Sapa hotel may use the elegant INSIDER TIPP *Victoria Express (return ticket from 3,250,000 dong | journey time 8–9 hrs | www.victoriahotels-asia.com).* There are also regular daily services to Lao Cai. Then take a scheduled bus or tourist coach on to Sapa.

SIGHTSEEING

HILL VILLAGE AND WATERFALLS
Easy walks via suspension bridges and through terraced paddy fields lead into the surrounding countryside, e.g. to the impressive ● *Cat Cat waterfall* (approx. 3km/2mi to the west) in a bamboo forest and to the *Thac Bac* or Silver Waterfall (approx. 10km/6mi to the west), which drops from about 100m (320ft) in three stages. The walks pass through the villages of the hill tribes, where there is accommodation – e.g. in *Ta Phin* (Village of the Red Dao) – or else you can take a stroll through the delightful *Ta Van* valley into the village of *Ta Van.* In the village of *Cat Cat*, near to the waterfall and so very much on the tourist trail, you can watch the Hmong women at work on their weaving and embroidery. Blue dresses and turban-style headwear are the char-

acteristic features of Hmong clothing, which they still make themselves and then dye with indigo.

MARKETS

The *weekend market* attracts countless visitors every Saturday. It may be smaller and attract fewer visitors, but the same market, with stalls run by the hill tribe minorities, is also held during the week. There are equally lively markets in the vicinity on other days. Mainly women and young girls belonging to the Black Hmong tribe wander the streets and alleys of Sapa, attempting to sell their hand-embroidered goods to tourists. Not only do they have a good command of French and English, they also deploy some sophisticated sales techniques.

FOOD & DRINK

MIMOSA

Hidden away at the top of a flight of steps on the main street. Seafood or wild boar, pasta or pizza, Vietnamese or vegetarian. You'll even find Nutella on the breakfast menu. *Cau May | tel. 020 3 87 13 77 | Budget*

The Thac Bac 'silver waterfall'

NATURE BAR & GRILL ●

Eat well in Vietnamese style (from the grill, vegetarian, even a little hint of Italian) by a warming hearth over a beer, a cocktail or a punch – the perfect spot on a cold winter's evening. *24 Cau May (2nd floor) | tel. 020 3 87 20 94 | Moderate*

TOP MOUNTAIN VIEW BAR ☼

Great panoramic view from the 4th floor of the Chaulong Sapa Hotel, plus a fine selection of drinks and cocktails. *24 Dong Loi | Moderate*

SPORTS & ACTIVITIES

The *Fan Si Pan* (Phan Si Pang), at 3,143m (10,300ft) Vietnam's highest mountain, is sometimes described as the 'roof of Indochina'. It is situated in the north of ☉ *Hoang Lien Son Nature Reserve*, known mainly for its varied range of bird species. Trekking tourists can climb to its summit in three- or five-day tours, but given the cold and damp climate and the sometimes overgrown tracks across rickety bamboo bridges, it is an excursion that only experienced mountainclimbers with porters and tents suitable for extreme conditions should undertake. The best time to make the climb up the 14km (9mi) path (in some places it is extremely steep) is between mid-October and mid-November and the end of February/early March to April, when the orchids and rhododendron are in flower *(further information: www.sapatravel.com).*

WHERE TO STAY

INSIDER TIPP **BAGUETTE & CHOCOLAT**
You can stay the night in one of this guesthouse's four tiny, but very nice rooms.

Supports an aid project for children. Also highly recommended is the welcoming restaurant with fireplace. *Thac Bac | tel. 020 3 87 17 66 | www.hoasua school.com | Budget*

BAMBOO SAPA ☼

Comfortable rooms (some with balcony and mock-fireplace, mountain panorama included) in this three-storey hotel. Also a good travel agency on the premises. *45 rooms | Cau May | tel. 020 3 87 10 75 | www.sapatravel.com | Moderate*

BOOKS & FILMS

▶ **Sunday Menu** – A collection of short stories told from the point of view of a young Vietnamese woman, Pham Thi Hoai, about everyday life in Hanoi in the 1990s.

▶ **The Girl in the Picture: the Story of Kim Phuc, the Photograph and the Vietnam War** by Denise Chong. An account of Vietnamese and American relationships during the Vietnam War through the eyes of the girl burnt in a napalm attack, as captured in a disturbing picture by AP photographer Nick Ut

▶ **The quiet American** – A remake (2002) of Graham Greene's classic (directed by Phillip Noyce). Set during the Indochina war, the British correspondent competes with a mysterious American for his beautiful lover, Phuong. Partly filmed in Hoi An

▶ **The Lover** was a Goncourt prize-winning novel by Marguerite Duras, who was born in what was then Indo-

china. The film was made in 1991 by Jean-Jacques Annaud as the erotic story of a 15-year-old French girl and an older, wealthy Vietnamese man

▶ **Cyclo** – a young man struggling to earn a living with his bicycle-taxi in Saigon meets a group of criminals, who introduce him to a mafia-style world of drugs and crime (1995)

▶ **Good morning Vietnam** – A film from 1978 demonstrates the absurdity of war. Robin Williams in the leading role as a DJ for the US armed services radio statio in Saigon. Directed by Barry Levinson

▶ **Apocalypse Now** – Oscar-winning film (1979) about the Vietnam war (Directed by Francis Ford Coppola). Often forgotten: Marlon Brando plays the psychopathic Colonel Kurtz

▶ Other films about the Vietnam War include **Platoon** (1986)**, We Were Soldiers** (2002) and **Rescue Dawn** (2007)

Green, blue, red, violet – traditional clothing in Bac Ha market

THAI BINH SAPA

Nice, family-run hotel on the outskirts, but quiet and warm (electric blankets, fireplace). Tours and guides. *14 rooms | 5 Ham Rong | tel. 020 3 87 12 12 | www.thaibinhhotel.com | Budget*

TOPAS ECOLODGE ☼ ☺

Lots of natural materials, solar energy and waste-water treatment. This is a Danish-Vietnamese hotel, where guests stay in rustic-style, but very comfortable mountain chalets. Plus a stunning panorama from above the clouds. Stay here for several nights, and the chance of enjoying the fantastic view increases, as mist is a regular occurrence in the winter. *25 rooms | 24 Muong Hoa | Thanh Kim (approx. 15km/9mi) southeast of Sapa, 45 mins on a gravel track) | tel. 020 3 87 13 31 | www.topasecolodge.com | Moderate*

VICTORIA SAPA ☼

One of Vietnam's top hotels, if not the best. In rustic chalet style, on the outskirts. The rooms are comfortable, some with four-poster bed and balcony. Other amenities include tennis court, badmin-

ton and a heated indoor pool. *76 rooms | tel. 020 3 87 15 22 | www.victoriahotels-asia.com | Expensive*

INFORMATION

Sapa Tourism | 2 Fansipan (on the way out of town towards the Cat Cat waterfall) | Sapa | tel. 020 3 87 19 75 | sapatourism@hn.vnn.vn | www.sapa-tourism.com

WHERE TO GO

BAC HA (132 C1) (⌀ D2)

This small town (pop. 3,000) lies about 100km (60mi) northeast of Sapa at an altitude of 900m (2,950ft). It's a part of the country famed for its *tam hoa* plums. In the spring the countryside is a blaze of white fruit tree blossom. A lively *market* forming a sea of green, blue, red and violet draws tourists in on Sunday. It now seems to attract even more visitors than those in Sapa. Everyone wants to see and photograph the 'flower Hmong' *(Hmong Hua)*, so called because of their multi-coloured clothing adorned with floral motifs.

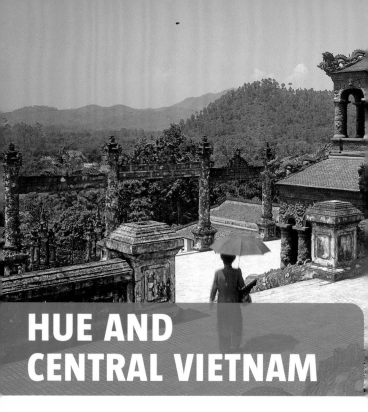

HUE AND CENTRAL VIETNAM

The central region of Vietnam around the resort of Da Nang has no fewer than three Unesco World Heritage sites – in addition to the old Imperial city of Hue, there are the enchanting ruins of the Champa complex in My Son (4th–13th century) and the largely Chinese market town of Hoi An, from the 17th century onwards an internationally important trading port by the South China Seas.

With its Imperial citadel by the Song Huong, the Perfume River, and impressive Imperial tombs, Hue is undoubtedly what attracts most visitors to this region. The many artisan villages around Hue are steeped in tradition. During the 19th century under the Nguyen dynasty, the arts and crafts flourished as never before. Many villagers earned a good living from painting, weaving, ceramics, and silverware, all important elements in the decorative ornamentation of the palaces, tombs and pagodas.

Always visible in central Vietnam is the Truong Son mountain range that runs parallel to the south coast for 1,000km (600mi). At no other point are the mountains closer to the sea than where the Bach Ma mountains form the dividing line between the subtropical north and the tropical south. If the region around Hue should live up to its reputation as the wettest in Vietnam, then you will simply have to make for Da Nang further south, where it is usually sunny. The port city is famous for its beaches, such as China Beach, and also the excellent Cham Museum, which sheds light on the ancient civilisation that

Photo: Tomb of Emperor Khai Dinh near Hue

The Imperial Palace at Hue, white beaches and Hoi An's Old Quarter – there are many different sides to the central part of Vietnam

once flourished here. During the Vietnam War, the magnificent Marble Mountains above Da Nang became a hide-out for the Viet Cong guerrillas. Such proximity to the US barracks gave the Americans goods reasons to be fearful.

One third of residents in Hoi An are Chinese, and their entrepreneurial flair is still very much in evidence, particularly in the markets. The narrow streets in the old quarter are lined with single-story Chinese trading houses, with colourful colonnades, pagodas and temples, but its character is changing – now increasingly art galleries, souvenir shops, tailors, bars and cafés also form part of the backdrop. On the border with south Vietnam the uplands broaden out to the west. Thanks to its location at an altitude of 1,500m (4,900ft) and a benign climate, Dalat is often justifiably described to as the 'City of Eternal Spring'. No surprise then that in recent years, this highland resort, and the last outpost of central Vietnam, has become very popular with honeymooners and golf tourists from Saigon.

BUON MA THUOT

(137 E1) (𝗆 G10) This city, with a population of 200,000 inhabitants, grew out of a French military station first established in 1910.

It's hard to identify where exactly the city centre is, but the heart of the town is largely a grid pattern of streets intersect-

ditional costumes, implements, hunting weapons and fishing tackle. *Wed–Sun 7am–11am, 2am–5pm | 182 Nguyen Du/ corner of Le Duan | admission approx. 10,000 dong*

FOOD & DRINK

BON TRIEU RESTAURANT
Try the delicious *bon bay mon* – wafer-thin beef in sweet'n sour sauces. *33 Hai Ba Trung | no telephone | Moderate*

Swing high – an elephant ride on Lake Lak

ing at right-angles. Many villas have survived from the days of the French occupation, when the officer class chose the cooler uplands, at about 500m (1,650ft) above sea level, as their summer retreat. Buon Ma Thuot is the provincial capital of Dak Lak and is renowned for its coffee, generally considered to be the best in Vietnam.

SIGHTSEEING

MUSEUM OF ETHNOLOGY
The rich culture of the Ede, Hmong and Muong hill tribes is explored in this fascinating museum. Displays include tra-

SHOPPING

INSIDER TIPP ▶ THAN BAO COFFEE SALES
The plantations around Buon Ma Thot yield very good and comparatively inexpensive coffee. You can buy whole beans or have them ground for you. *Hoang Dieu*

WHERE TO STAY

DAM SAN HOTEL
The best hotel in town. Modern rooms, garden pool, tennis court. Some nice cafés nearby. *60 rooms | 212 Nguyen Cong Tru | tel. 0500 3 85 12 34 | www.damsan hotel.com.vn | Budget–Moderate*

DAKRUCO HOTEL

This modern, very comfortable hotel is easily visible. It has large and well-equipped rooms (including wi-fi), some with balcony, but is noisy on the street side and often full of wedding guests. Small pool, spa, tennis court. *114 rooms | 30 Nguyen Chi Thanh | tel. 0500 3 97 08 88 | www.dakrucohotels.com | Moderate*

INFORMATION

Dak Lak Tourist | 53 Ly Thuong Kiet | tel. 0500 3 85 22 46 | www.daklaktourist.com.vn

WHERE TO GO

Until World War II, the province of Dak Lak was used by the emperor as his hunting grounds – that's no surprise, as there's no other region in Vietnam with such a plentiful supply of game. There is also plenty of water. Some 27km (17mi) southwest of Buon Ma Thuot, the cascading *Drai Sap falls* (137 E1) *(ጠ G10)* in the heart of a rainforest are an impressive sight, especially after heavy rainfall.

In *Buon Tua* (Bon Tur) you can get to meet members of the Ede hill tribe. Also known as the Rhade, here mothers are heads of family. And the clans live in longhouses.

Storks, cranes and ducks exploit the perfect habitat beside Lake *Lak* (137 E2) *(ጠ G11)* (approx. 50km/30mi south of Buon Ma Thuot).

Go to the Muong village of *Buon Jun* (also Ban Jun) and you can take INSIDER TIPP a ride on an elephant – an extraordinary experience, and one enjoyed not only by families with children. *Ban Don* (137 E1) *(ጠ G10),* approx. 45km (28mi) northwest of Buon Ma Thuot, is another place where you can ride out on a pachyderm *(approx. 2,000,000 dong per hour, further information and booking with Dak Lak Tourist in Buon Ma Thuot).* In Ban Don the Muong minority still trap wild elephants, tame them and then use them for transporting timber.

⭐ **Dalat**
The lovers' city oozes colonial charm, while the surrounding area is a haven for active holidaymakers → p. 58

⭐ **Po Klong Garai towers**
The Cham perfected the art of temple construction → p. 59

⭐ **Cham Museum**
Relics from an ancient culture in Da Nang → p. 61

⭐ **My Son**
A Unesco Heritage Site in the middle of the jungle – the ruins of the Cham's temple complex → p. 63

⭐ **Marble Mountains**
Mysterious caves and pagodas, incense sticks and souvenirs – plus a fantastic all-round view from the top of Mount Thuy Son → p. 63

⭐ **Hoi An**
Picturesque rows of streets, trading houses and pagodas in the Old Quarter, plus large helpings of Mediterranean-style charm → p. 64

⭐ **Hue citadel**
By the Perfume River – see for yourself the opulence and grandeur enjoyed by Vietnam's former rulers on a stroll through the site → p. 70

MARCO POLO HIGHLIGHTS

DALAT

(137 E2) (*🗺 G11*) ⭐ **Dalat (pop. 200,000) is variously described as the favourite spot for home-sick Europeans, tourist hotspot and honeymoon capital for Vietnamese newly-weds.**

The latter is due mainly to the fact that young Vietnamese couples regard lakes, waterfalls and forests as the epitome of romance. When in the spring, after the Tet festival, the cherry trees are in full pink blossom, the setting is perfect – the only downside being that it rains frequently here. It was in 1897 that the doctor Alexandre Yersin founded a sanatorium in this city, which sits at an altitude of 1,475m (4,800ft). It was another 15 years before the first Europeans settled here. For the upper echelons of colonial society the smart Palace Hotel was the perfect place to spend the hot summer months. Those who could afford it, including the last Vietnamese emperor, Bao Dai, built villas in the pine forests above the Xuan Huong reservoir, where water levels are unfortunately now running low. The favourite pursuit of the wealthy summer visitors was hunting tigers and elephants in what was at that time dense forest.

SIGHTSEEING

CHUA THIEN VUONG

The three yellow timber pagodas, built in 1958 by the Chaozhou Chinese community, stand on a hill surrounded by pine forests. Of particular interest here are the three approx. 4-m (13-ft) high Buddha statues, which were donated by British Buddhists from Hong Kong. They are made from gilded sandalwood and each one weighs around 1400kg (3000lb). *Approx. 5km (3mi) southeast of the city centre, via Khe San street.*

SUMMER PALACE (DINH III) ●

A yellow-brown villa with about 26 rooms, built in 1933, recalls the days of Bao Dai, Vietnam's last emperor, who ruled from 1926 to 1945. On display here are the Imperial living rooms and many private photos. *Daily 7am–11am, 1.30pm–4pm | 2 Le Hong Phong | admission 10,000 dong*

FOOD & DRINK

PHUONG HOANG

Try some of the delicious Vietnamese specialities, such as marinated meat grilled at the table. *81 Phan Dinh Phung | tel. 063 3 82 27 73 | Budget*

THUY TA RESTAURANT 🍴

The restaurant occupies a magnificent spot – on stilts by Lake Xuan Huong. The view from here on sunny afternoons is just perfect. *1 Yersin | tel. 063 3 82 22 88 | Moderate–Expensive*

SPORTS & ACTIVITIES

BIKING, TREKKING, FUN SPORTS

The pretty countryside and the pleasant climate provide just the right conditions for outdoor adventure – cycle tours (approx. 50,000 dong per day), a climb to the top of 🍴 *Mount Lang Bian* (with detours to the Lat villages), trekking, rock climbing, abseiling, paragliding and canyoning are just some of the options. Always check equipment and mountain bikes very carefully beforehand. One recommended tour operator is *Phat Tire Ventures | 109 Nguyen Van Troi | tel. 063 3 82 94 22 | mobile 09 18 43 87 81 | www. phattireventures.com.*

DALAT PALACE GOLF CLUB

The 18-hole course and the magnificent hilly scenery attract tournament golfers from all over the world. *Phu Dong Thien Vuong | tel. 063 3 82 12 01 and 3 82 35 07 | www.dalatpalacegolf.vn | Green fee package from approx. 2,200,000 dong on weekdays with hotel accommodation*

WHERE TO STAY

ANA MANDARA VILLAS DALAT & SPA
Magnificently restored colonial villas with discretely elegant furnishings and décor, heated pool, wine cellar, exclusive restaurant. It could hardly be more luxurious. *57 rooms | Le Lai | tel. 063 3 55 58 88 | www.anamandara-resort.com | Expensive*

DALAT PALACE ☀
A combination of luxury and nostalgia recalling the grandeur of the 1920s. Plus a great view over Lake Xuan Huong. *43 rooms | 12 Tran Phu | tel. 063 3 82 54 44 | www.dalatpalace.vn | Expensive*

INSIDER TIPP ▶ NGOC LAN HOTEL ☀
An old cinema has been transformed into a large, mid-range hotel with smart rooms, some of which are huge (parquet floors) and have magnificent balcony views over the lake. The smaller rooms at the rear are quieter. Massage and fitness suite, superb location near the market. Try asking for a discount! *91 rooms | 42 Nguyen Chi Thanh | tel. 063 3 83 88 38 | www.ngoclanhotel.vn | Moderate*

INFORMATION

Dalat Tourist | No. 7 in Road 3 Thang 2 | tel. 063 3 82 24 79 | www.dalattourist. com.vn

WHERE TO GO

PO KLONG GARAI TOWERS ★
(137 F3) *(Ø H11)*
Spiky cacti surround the four chunky Cham towers of Po Klong Garai, situated approx. 65km (40mi) southeast of Dalat on the N 20 to Phan Rang. The best time to visit is September/October, when to celebrate their new year the Cham perform traditional songs and dances at the site. What is so surprising is the good

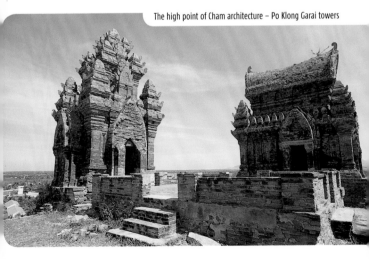

The high point of Cham architecture – Po Klong Garai towers

condition of the buildings – the temples were built in the 13/14th century during the regency of King Simhavarman III. You enter the temple complex through a beautifully decorated gateway in the middle of the perimeter wall. Adorning the inside the temple tower is a mukha lingam, a stylised phallus symbolising Shiva. *Daily 7.30am–6pm | admission 5,000 dong*

WATERFALLS (137 E2) (*G11*)

Leaving from the old station in Dalat, approx. 500m east of Lake Xuan Huong, a train runs several times a day (morning and midday) to the Linh Phuoc Pagoda in the town of *Trai Mat*. From here there is 7-km (4-mi) signposted trail to the beautiful *Tiger waterfall (Thac Hang Cop | admission 5,000 dong)*, where you will be greeted by a huge statue of a tiger. Unfortunately, not just the waterfalls, but also the town lakes, are suffering badly from the high demands of the vast Da Nhim reservoir further west. The cascades are most impressive at the end of the rainy period (Nov/Dec). Other good examples include the *Prenn waterfall (by the N 20, approx. 10km/6mi from Dalat)*, the *Lien Khuong* waterfall *(N 20, approx. 30km/20mi towards Saigon)*, the *Pong-our* waterfall by the N 20 *(45km/28mi towards Saigon)* and the huge *Dambri* waterfall near Bao Loc.

DA NANG

(135 E3) (*G7*) **On the section of road from Hue to Da Nang you will notice a distinct change in the climate once you have negotiated Cloud Pass (Deo Hai Van).** Warmer and drier air takes over as you descend from Mount Bach Ma (White Horse Mountain) to the picturesque coastline. You will soon reach Da Nang, the rapidly growing provincial capital of approx. 1.1 million inhabitants. Because

Impressive natural spectacle – Pongour waterfall near Dalat

CITY WHERE TO START?
Savour the atmosphere on Da Nang's lively **Bach Dang Promenade** beside the River Han; then head north from the Cham Museum, past old villas, hotels, the market and the tourist information office. Everything is easily accessible on foot – if you're coming from a beach hotel, take a (moped) taxi

it occupies a favourable location at the mouth of the River Han, Da Nang has always been an important port. The Spanish landed here in the 17th century, the French in the 19th century. Later on, the Americans occupied the town and set about developing what was to become one of their largest air bases in southeast Asia. Despite all the destruction wrought by the war, Da Nang has a fine promenade overlooked by mature trees and grand villas dating from the French colonial era. They have recently been renovated and are now very smart. China Beach is renowned for its high waves – during the war American soldiers came here to surf when they had 'rest and relaxation' time.

SIGHTSEEING

CAO DAI TEMPLE ●

Like the Holy See in Tay Ninh, the Cao Dai Temple here, the second-largest in the country, is an impressive sight. Access is strictly segregated by sex. Women enter the shrine on the left, men on the right. Priests are allowed to use the central entrance. Behind the altar the 'divine eye' made from a huge glass ball watches the faithful at prayer. *Services daily at 6am, noon, 6pm and midnight | near the station | admission free*

CHAM MUSEUM ★ ●

Founded in 1915 by the French, this small, but rather fine, Cham Museum, houses the world's best collection of Cham artefacts, many of which are sandstone sculptures. You should set aside at least two hours to cover what is a clearly arranged set of displays. You probably won't have

Sandstone relief from the collection in Da Nang's Cham Museum

time to see everything, but make sure you include the mythical Hindu bird, Garuda, statues of the elephant-headed god, Ganesha, and of the trinity, Brahma, Vishnu and Shiva. Eight hundred years of civilisation are skilfully compressed into a tiny space. *Daily 7am–5.30pm | near the Nu Vuong junction / Bach Dang | admission approx. 40,000 dong*

CATHEDRAL

The church built by the French in 1923 is today used by over 4,000 Catholic worshippers in Da Nang. Note the rather neat medieval-style, stained-glass windows. *North of the Cham Museum in Tran Phu.*

The best time for swimming is from April to August. A very popular beach is the pretty INSIDER TIPP *Canh Duong Beach* near Lang Co approx. 20km (12mi) north of Da Nang. Considered to be one of Vietnam's finest, it is about 8km (5mi) in length.

FOOD & DRINK

COOL SPOT

This is the bar where back-packers come to sit with a beer and a snack to catch up on the news back home, either by reading the western newspapers or by watching the satellite TV channels. *112 Tran Phu | tel. 0511 3 82 40 40 | Moderate*

INSIDER TIPP TRUC LAM VIEN (GARDEN VIEW CAFÉ)

Bamboo garden retreat in Imperial style. Vietnamese and Chinese specialities, noodle soups, hot pots and other classics, plus delicious seafood, buffet at the weekend and a western breakfast with good coffee and cappuccinos. *8 Tran Quy Cap | tel. 0511 3 58 24 28 | www.truclam vien.com.vn | Budget–Moderate*

WATERFRONT

A smart and airy bar-restaurant with stunning river view from 2nd floor terrace. International and Vietnamese food, good wine list, lots of cocktails, attentive waiting staff. Live band on Monday. *150–152 Bach Dang | tel. 0511 3 84 33 73 | Moderate–Expensive*

BEACHES

China Beach, a popular spot with tourists, extends south from the Mount Son Tra (Monkey Mountain) for about 30km (19mi). But take care as there are sometimes dangerous currents in these waters.

WHERE TO STAY

DAI A HOTEL

This small hotel occupies a central position in the town near to the river. The rooms are relatively simple, but they do have internet access. Breakfast and collection from the airport included. *34 rooms | 51 Yen Bai | tel. 0511 3 82 75 32 | www.daiahotel.com.vn | Budget*

THE FURAMA RESORT

This complex inspired by the Imperial architecture of Hue boasts luxurious, elegant villas, beautifully laid-out gardens, lagoons and top-class sports facilities. One of Vietnam's top hotels. *200 rooms | 68 Ho Xuan | Bac My An (China Beach) | tel. 0511 3 84 78 88 | www. furamavietnam.com | Expensive*

SANDY BEACH RESORT

Large beach hotel by the delightful Non Nuoc beach with bright rooms and bungalows, two pools and tennis courts. *124 rooms | 255 Huyen Tran Cong Chua | Hoa Hai, Ngu Hanh Son district | tel. 0511 3 83 62 16 | www.sandybeachdanang.com | Expensive*

INFORMATION

Saigon Tourist Da Nang | 357 Phan Chu Trinh | tel. 0511 3 89 72 29 and 3 82 72 11 | www.saigontouristdanang.com | www. danang.gov.vn

WHERE TO GO

MARBLE MOUNTAINS ⭐
(135 E3) (*ᴓ G7*)

Situated just over 8km (5mi) south of Da Nang and rising steeply from a plain near China Beach is a cluster of five 'mountains' up to 100m (320ft) in height. They are named after the five elements of Chinese philosophy: thuy (water), tho (earth), kim (metal), moc (wood) and moa (fire). According to legend, the mountains are eggs laid by a giant dragon. The most famous of the five is *Thuy Son*, the water mountain; from the ⚜ *Vong Giac Dai* viewpoint at the summit, there's a stunning panorama extending over the beach, the sea and other mountains. You can make a circular tour lasting about an hour (torch and mosquito repellent spray essential) to explore the caverns formerly used by the Cham. Particularly impressive are the *Tam Tai Pagoda* and the approx. 30-m (100-ft) high *Huyen Khong Cave*, where you will find countless incense sticks burning by the statue of Thich Ca (Buddha of the Present Moment). A calm, almost magical, aura exists, as golden rays of sunlight shine through the roof of the cave, while worshippers are bowed in prayer in front of the Buddha. From *Tang Chon*, the last cave, a path leads down the *Linh Ung Pagoda* and into the village of *Quang Nam*, where the locals sell marble souvenirs. *Marble Mountains daily 7am–5pm | admission 25,000 dong*

MY SON ⭐ (135 D–E3) (*ᴓ G7*)

Some 32km (20mi) south of Da Nang, a narrow road branches off to *Nong Son*. Suddenly, emerging from the dense jungle vegetation, are a series of mossy rust-red temple towers overgrown with green ferns. From the 4th to the 13th century, My Son was the Cham's most important religious and cultural centre. The founding of the shrine, dedicated to the God Shiva, is attributed to the Champa king, Bhadravarman, whose power base was in present-day Tra Kieu, some 20km (12mi) to the east. In the

Keeping watch in Huyen Khong Cave

7th century, work started on replacing the sacred buildings, originally made of wood, with brick structures. No mortar or lime was used in their construction; remarkably, resin from the cau day tree held the walls together.

For many tourists, My Son is just another collection of forgotten ruins – towers, walls and temples, many of which suffered badly during the Vietnam War. Once the Viet Cong discovered the valley, considering it to be a safe hiding-place, the US Army declared the region a 'free fire zone'. Only a fraction of the originally 70 sacred buildings survived the bombardment undamaged. But if you have studied the story behind the Champa kingdom in depth, then you can't pass My Son by. In 1999 Unesco rightly declared the entire temple complex a World Heritage Site.

The Cham temples beneath Mount My Son (Beautiful Mountain) are divided into four groups: Group A consists of stone reliefs, Group B a splendid gateway opening on to the shrine. The brick walls in the Group C buildings show predominantly Cham motifs and Group D is an ensemble of six buildings and the stele courtyard with votive panels. Please note: countless landmines were laid around My Son and they are still live, so under no circumstances should you deviate from the marked trails. *Daily 6.30am–4.30pm | admission 80,000 dong*

HOI AN

(135 E3) (*ʲʲ G7*) ★ **A unique marriage of Mediterranean-style elegance and the exotic charm of the Far East.**

As you stroll through the picturesque alleys of Hoi An, it's hard to imagine that some 300 years ago this town (pop. 80,000) was one of the most important ports in southeast Asia. It was established by the Cham and then extended by the Nguyen rulers. Over time, the size of cargo vessels increased and it was then no longer necessary for stopovers in smaller harbours, so in the early part of the 19th century, Hoi An went into decline. Only in the 1990s, when tourism brought a revival did the town's fortunes improve.

The consequences of this rapid development are visible everywhere. There are hardly any more general stores; outsiders have moved in and transformed the town into a collection of souvenir shops, restaurants and small hotels. Fortunately, Hoi An has retained its reputation as the Vietnam's 'tailor town'. You can get measured up in the morning and be wearing a fine silk suit or dress in the evening.

OLD QUARTER

The Old Quarter covers the area from between the Bach Dang promenade and Phan Chu Trinh – if you take a stroll around the town, you will be taken aback by the number of historic trading houses, commercial buildings, assembly halls and pagodas.

Unesco listed the town centre as a World Heritage Site in 1999 and as a result more than 800 buildings are subject to preservation orders. The houses belonging to the Chinese community are particularly exotic. The Heavenly Empress, Thien Hau, who watches over the fortunes of seafarers, is worshipped in the Phu Kien Pagoda in the Fujian Chinese assembly hall. Also of interest are the ornate carvings in the house of the Chaozhou Chinese, which dates from 1776.

An admission ticket is required if you wish to explore the historic buildings; a

Richly ornamented Chinese assembly hall in Hoi An

collective ticket is valid for five entries. Costing 100,000 dong, they are available from one of several sales points in the Old Quarter, e.g. opposite *Hoi Quan Phuoc Kien* (the Fujian Chinese assembly hall) at *47 Tran Phu*.

If possible, try to time your visit for the **INSIDER TIPP** *Hoi An Legendary Night*. Every month on the night before the full moon festival (14th day of the lunar calendar), the narrow, moonlit lanes in the Old Quarter are illuminated by fairy lights, candles and colourful lanterns. The townsfolk spend Legendary Night in the old houses, listening to folk music, readings and sharing local delicacies.

TRADING HOUSES

Most of the commercial properties in the town date from the early 19th century. Today they are used for ancestor worship, business and family life. Probably the finest is *Quan Thang House (77 Tran Phu)* with its striking green tile roof. *Phung Hung House (4 Nguyen Thi Minh Khai)* has decorative shutters and a suspended ancestral altar. For more than 200 years,

generations of a single clan have lived in *Tan Ky House (daily 8am–5.30pm | 101 Nguyen Thai Hoc)*. Note the intricate filigree carvings. Another house to include in your five entries is the Chapel of the *Tran Family (daily 7am–6pm | 21 Phan Chu Trinh)*, where there are some fine ivory carvings. *Diep Dong Nguyen House (80 Nguyen Thai Hoc)* was formerly a trading office for Chinese medicines and herbal remedies. *Opening times usually 8am–5pm or 8am–6pm*

JAPANESE BRIDGE

In Hoi An the Chinese and the Japanese communities had their own quarters, with the boundary line between the two zones an 18-m (60-ft) long, covered Japanese bridge. Work on the first bridge (subsequently destroyed several times) started in 1593 in the Chinese Year of the Monkey, as is indicated by the two monkeys on the Japanese side of the bridge. Two years later, the wooden structure with a roof of green and yellow tiles was finished in the Year of the Dog. Note the two stone dogs on the Chinese side.

Breakfast Vietnamese-style – noodle soup in Hoi An

FOOD & DRINK

The small restaurants and bars by the river on *Nguyen Hue, Tran Phu* and *Bach Dang* are cheerful places to eat or enjoy a drink after a day's sightseeing. Do try INSIDER TIPP *cao lau,* a tasty soup of noodles, pork and green vegetables, prepared with water from Hoi An's ancient spring.

INSIDER TIPP BROTHER'S CAFÉ HOI AN

In an idyllic spot on a quiet street by the Thu Bon river. Relax in a colonial villa with a tropical garden, airy wooden interior and exposed beams and enjoy good Vietnamese or international cuisine. Well-stocked wine cellar. Book your table for the evening meal. *27 Phan Boi Chau | tel. 0510 3 91 41 50 | www.brother cafehoian.com | Expensive*

LIGHTHOUSE CAFÉ & RESTAURANT

For the best view of the Old Quarter, get a table in this two-storey restaurant on the other side of the river, on Cam Nam island. A number of Hoi An classics, plus western-style dishes and wines from all over the world. Also on offer: cycle tours into rural Hoi An and cookery lessons. *Tho 5, Thon Xuyen Trung | Cam Nam | tel. 0510 3 93 62 35 | www.lighthousecafe hoian.com | free shuttle boats (marked Hai Dang) until approx. 9pm | Moderate*

INSIDER TIPP RED BRIDGE RESTAURANT

It's worth dining out in this rural, open-air restaurant for the 20-minute boat trip alone ... and then the return journey by moonlight. Modern Vietnamese cuisine in an elegant setting by the banks of the river. *Daily 8am–5pm, free shuttle boat daily at noon, in the evening only for groups of five or more with reservation, on the waterfront (74 Bach Dang, opposite Café Can), collection also from the hotel pier | Thon 4 | Cam Thanh (approx. 4km/2.5mi from the town centre, signposted) | tel. 0510 3 93 32 22 | www. visithoian.com | Moderate*

SHOPPING

Hoi An is famed for its bespoke tailoring service and for silk, most of which comes from China. One metre of natural silk, 90cm wide, costs approx. 250,000 dong.

HOI AN HANDICRAFT WORKSHOP
For souvenirs, crafts and performances of traditional music. *9 Nguyen Thai Hoc*

QUYNH GIAO
Mrs Quynh sells lovely ceramics in unusual designs. She will also ship her work by sea or by air. Her shop at *683 Hai Ba Trung* also sells silk paintings. *681 Hai Ba Trung | qgiao2000@hotmail.com*

REACHING OUT
Disabled artisans make and sell some beautiful items in this historic building (e.g. handbags, jewellery, clothing, toys). *103 Nguyen Thai Hoc | near the Tan Ky house | www.reachingoutvietnam.com*

SILK ROAD
Good Old Quarter boutique where tailor Thuy magics up blouses, clothes and trousers from 200,000 dong, depending on material and size. *91 Nguyen Thai Hoc | tel. 0510 3 91 10 58 | silkroadvn@ hotmail.com*

THOI TRANG
This tailor is rather more expensive than the others, but is very reliable and uses good quality material. Guide prices: a pair of trousers costs approx. 350,000 dong, a suit from 500,000 dong, a blouse between 150,000 and 200,000 dong. *73 Tran Phu | tel. 0510 3 86 10 40*

LEISURE, SPORTS & BEACH

BOAT TOURS
Take a tour along the Thu Bon river on one of the paddle boat tours and explore the artisan and fishing villages in the vicinity *(one-hour tours cost approx. 50,000 dong)*.

COOKERY COURSES ●
It's the latest trend. Many restaurants now offer cookery courses, some with visit to the market included, e.g. *Vy's Cooking School in the Morning Glory (106*

Boat trips start here – landing stage on the Thu Bon river

Nguyen Thai Hoc | tel. 0510 2 24 15 56 | www.restaurant-hoian.com), Brothers Café, Red Bridge Restaurant and *Tam Tam.*

BEACH

The fine-sand *Cua Dai beach* is really just a southern extension of China Beach. Only 5km (3mi) from Hoi An. *Cua Dai (extension of Tran Hung Dao)*

ENTERTAINMENT

If you fancy an evening stroll, then the Bach Dang waterfront is ideal.

CHAMPA BAR

Popular with tourists and locals alike. *Daily approx. 11am–11pm | 75–77 Nguyen Thai Hoc | tel. 0510 3 86 29 74*

TAM TAM

1000 CDs, good mojitos; sit on the balcony and follow events on the lively street below. *Daily approx. 8am–11pm | 110 Nguyen Thai Hoc | tel. 0510 3 86 22 12*

WHERE TO STAY

CUA DAI HOTEL

A little gem in colonial-style – quiet, nicely-decorated rooms with rattan furniture, some with balcony, welcoming lobby, pool in garden. Good breakfast, 15 minutes on foot to the Old Quarter. *24 rooms | 544 Cua Dai | tel. 0510 3 86 22 31 | www.cuadai-hoian.com | Moderate*

LIFE HERITAGE RESORT HOI AN

This stylish, three-storey hotel in neo-colonial style has smart, spacious rooms (if perhaps rather gloomy on the lower floors) with small terrace to the garden or to the river. Own pier, large pool and spa. *94 rooms | 1 Phan Hong Thai | tel. 0510 3 91 45 55 | www.life-resorts.com | Expensive*

INSIDER TIPP ► LONG LIFE HOTEL

Excellent value for money – stylishly furnished, bright, quiet rooms, some with balcony overlooking the garden and rice paddy, beautiful bathroom with corner bath-tub, friendly staff, pool. Book in good time. *20 rooms | 30 Ba Trieu | tel. 0510 3 91 66 96 | www.longlifehotels.com | Moderate*

PALM GARDEN RESORT

On the outskirts of the town, but beside the quiet and beautiful Cua Dai beach (or more accurately, by Bang beach). Spacious bungalow hotel with large garden, pool, Italian restaurant, all bungalows with open-air bath tubs. Shuttle bus to Hoi An. *188 rooms | tel. 0510 3 92 79 27 | www.palmgardenresort.com.vn | Expensive*

VICTORIA HOI AN RESORT

Beautiful bungalow complex in old Hoi An style. The majority of the 100 rooms and suites open to the sea, the others to the river. Private beach, pool, tennis, fitness suite, water sports. *Cua Dai beach | tel. 0510 3 92 70 40 | www.victoriahotels-asia.com | Expensive*

INFORMATION

The Sinh Tourist | 587 Hai Ba Trung | tel. 0510 3 86 39 48 | www.thesinhtourist.vn

WHERE TO GO

Plenty of unspoilt beaches in the vicinity, but also many places of historical interest to explore, *e.g. Cham Towers,* the remains of Hindu temples. One such brick-built structure can be seen near *Bang An* (135 E3) (*Ø G7),* 10km (6mi) west of Hoi An. On the way there stop off in *Thanh Ha,* a pottery town. Only a few of the potters here sell direct to the public, those that do make products of good quality.

Ferries *(daily 7am, approx. 2-hour crossing)* link the mainland with the island of *Cham* (135 E3) *(ᗰ G7)*, which lies about 20km (12mi) offshore. It is famous for its swallows' nests, which are exported to China. Divers love it too. Not just because visibility during the dry season can be up to 30m (100ft), but you can also swim among a varied range of tropical fish.

Basic accommodation is available in the fishing village of *Tan Hiep*. Many visitors explore Cham Island as part of an organised tour.

HUE

(135 D3) *(ᗰ G7)* **Despite the still all too visible scars of the Vietnam War, the city of Hue with its 400,000 inhabitants still exudes peace and serenity. It's a place with a long and distinguished history that has seen many different rulers come and go.**

Not surprisingly the Vietnamese word hue means harmony. Hue was the capital of the last Imperial dynasty, the Nguyen, from 1802 to 1945. As the city lies at about halfway between Hanoi and Saigon, it has developed into an important hub for central Vietnam. Another factor that has contributed to the city's appeal include its idyllic situation straddling the Suong Huong (Perfume River), which flows at a sluggish pace flanked by gentle hills. A number of theories have been proposed for the origin of its evocative name, Perfume River. One suggestion refers to the sweet-smelling hardwood logs, which were once transported on the river, another that in the spring blossom lands on the surface of the water

Following the Chinese model – the Forbidden City in the citadel at Hue

and then floats downstream. Relics from the past here are the citadel with the Imperial City and the Imperial Palace, the Thien Mu Pagoda and the Imperial Tombs a few kilometres south of the city. Home to some of the country's leading universities, Hue has retained its importance as an administrative centre and a seat of learning. But not least come the outward-looking residents of Hue, who play their part in creating the city's welcoming atmosphere. The harmonious co-existence of past and present, upheaval and endurance, rural and urban culture all add to Hue's charm.

> ### 🏙 WHERE TO START?
> When you arrive in Hue, take a stroll along the **Huong Promenade**, past the park, the bridge, beautifully illuminated at night, the Saigon Morin colonial hotel and continue as far as the pier for the dragon boats. Everything is within walking distance. From here take dragon boat to the pagoda or cross to the Imperial City by taxi or cyclo

SIGHTSEEING

CITADEL ⭐

On the left bank of the Song Huong stands the 17th-century citadel, which was listed by Unesco as a World Heritage Site in 1993. It is surrounded by a walled enclosure some 10km (6mi) in length on ramparts 6m (20ft) high. In places this perimeter wall was 20m (65ft) thick. The citadel was once a state within a city, with temples, official apartments, decorative gardens and broad, shaded boulevards. Everything was laid out strictly in accordance with the rules of feng shui and subject to astrological calculations, so that the whole complex was in unison with nature. In fact it's like a set of nested boxes, i.e. a palace within a city within a citadel.

The finest part is the old Imperial Palace, the so-called Forbidden City, where the library, private reception rooms and temple halls are open to the public. Cross the *Phu Xuan Bridge* to reach the 37-m (120-ft) high *Flag Tower* dating from 1809. Flying from it on public holidays is the yellow flag of the Heavenly Dynasty. The sturdy *Ngo Mon Gate* (Noontime Gate) is the main way in to the Imperial City. In the past only the emperor was allowed to use this entrance. On top of the gate is the *Ngu Phung*, the brick-tiled *Five Phoenix*

Closed to the people for centuries – the gates in Hue

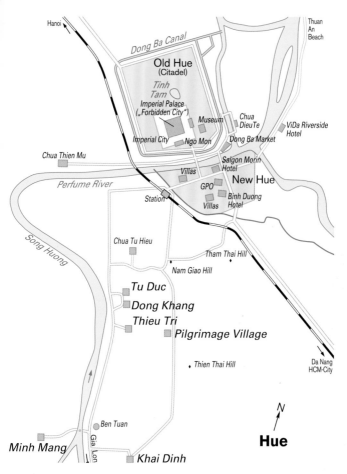

Hanoi

Dong Ba Canal

Old Hue
(Citadel)

Tinh
Tam

Imperial Palace
(„Forbidden City")

Chua
DieuTe

Museum

Imperial City

Ngo Mon

Dong Ba Market

ViDa Riverside
Hotel

Chua Thien Mu

Saigon Morin
Hotel

Villas

New Hue

Perfume River

GPO

Binh Duong
Hotel

Station

Villas

Thuan
An
Beach

Song Huong

Chua Tu Hieu

Tham Thai Hill

Nam Giao Hill

Tu Duc

Dong Khang

Thieu Tri

Pilgrimage Village

Thien Thai Hill

Da Nang
HCM-City

Ben Tuan

N

Gia Long

Minh Mang

Hue

Khai Dinh

Belvedere. This was where the emperor appeared on important occasions. Fittingly, it was also where the last Nguyen emperor announced his abdication in 1945. *Daily 7am–5pm | admission 55,000 dong* Cross a courtyard and the Golden Water Bridge *(Trung Dao)* to reach the Dien *Thai Hoa* throne palace, the Palace of Supreme Harmony. Note the dominant red and gold, the colours of the Imperial family. The emperor would sit on a magnificently carved, gilded throne in the centre of the hall. With nine stelae dividing up the two-level area, the Ceremonial Court was where the mandarins-in-waiting would stand according to their rank. Civilian officials stood to the right, top military brass on the left. Pass through the Golden Gateway *(Dai Cung Mon)* into the Palace of the Laws of Heaven, behind which stands the Imperial Palace proper. To the right and left of it in the Hall of Mandarins officials prepared for an audience with the emperor. Even today visitors must dress appropriately

Hats for rice farmers and souvenir hunters

before entering. Turn to the left and you will be standing in front of the emperor's private quarters. Eunuchs stood guard over the Imperial harem here.

Performances of folk music *(ca hue)* take place in the Duyen Thi Duong theatre in the morning and at lunch-time *(if a sufficient number of spectators are present, 9am, 10am, 2.30pm, 3.30pm, 50,000 dong)*.

Leave the Imperial city via the East Gate *(Hien Nhan Mon)* and head towards the museum complex. The interesting *Palace Museum* was installed in the former Long An Palace not far from the southeastern corner of the wall *(daily 7am–4.30pm | 3 Le Truc | admission 25,000 dong)*. It houses furniture, clothing, porcelain and decorative objects from the palace. It is worth a visit if only for a close look at the well-proportioned wooden structure. Its frame is made from very hard ironwood, while many carvings, including 35 poems and lines of prose, adorn the beams and windows.

FOOD & DRINK

ANCIENT HUE ●

Tourists eat like emperors here. This grand restaurant resembles an Imperial temple and serves food to match. Lush garden. You must try the nine-course Royal Dinner. *4/4/8 Lane 35 | Pham Thi Lien (near the Thien Mu Pagoda) | www. ancienthue.com.vn | Moderate–Expensive*

INSIDER TIPP ▶ CAFÉ VIOLON MUC DONG

A small pavilion of glass and bamboo by a lake. Classical concerts from 8pm, with small snacks, ice-cream and cocktails from the well-stocked bar. Mainly Vietnamese clientele. *6am until last customer leaves | 41A Hung Vuong | tel. 054 6 25 20 09 | Budget*

INSIDER TIPP ▶ CAFE ON THU WHEELS

A meeting-place for travellers. You can look forward not only to a proper breakfast, but also a good range of drinks. Long opening times a big draw. They also organise good motorcycle tours into the surrounding countryside. *10/2 Nguyen Tri Phuong | tel. 054 3 83 22 41 | Budget*

TROPICAL GARDEN

Garden restaurant for tourists in the hotel quarter. Folkloric shows every day. Come here to sample banh khoai, classic Vietnamese pancakes, and various other noodle dishes. *27 Chu Van An | tel. 054 3 84 71 43 | Budget–Moderate*

SHOPPING

Dong Ba market is the address if you fancy one of those typically Vietnamese rice straw hats. Southeast of the citadel on the left bank of the river.

On the opposite side of the river, there are various markets (fruit, vegetables, coffee) in *Phan Boi Chau, in Nguyen Con Tru (corner of Ba Trieu)* and in *Huong Vuong* near the bus station.

INSIDER TIPP ▶ VU NGOC STYLE

This young fashion designer, whose shop is in the traveller quarter, offers women a wide choice: flamboyant creations in glitter, fringe, sequin or pink feathers or traditional wraparound silk dresses in ao dai style. Customers with special requests can ask for a made-to-measure service. *25 Vo Thi Sau*

BEACH

Worth the 13km (8mi) journey is *Thuan An beach* by a pretty lagoon northeast of Hue. So far only the *Ana Mandara* hotel has opened here, but there are a few restaurants, loungers and parasols for beach boys and girls.

ENTERTAINMENT

BROWN EYES BAR

Popular club for the 18 to 25s. Western music and karaoke. *56 Chu Van An*

DMZ BAR

Popular with backpackers and resident expats. *Daily approx. 11am–11pm | 44 Le Loi | tel. 054 3 82 34 14*

WHERE TO STAY

ORCHID HOTEL

One of the best smaller hotels in the country, and not just in this price category. The main selling point for this hotel is its incredibly comfortable rooms and a helpful, friendly service (all rooms with laminate flooring, large beds, PC, TV, DVD, nice baths, fruit platter). INSIDER TIPP ▶ One super bargain is family room no. 601 with balcony (*Moderate*) or the (slightly tacky) *Romantic Room* for honeymooners (jacuzzi and honeymoon cake | *Moderate*). Make sure you book in good time. *18 rooms | 30 A Chu Van An | tel. 054 3 83 11 77 | www.orchidhotel.com. vn | Budget–Moderate*

PILGRIMAGE VILLAGE

Out of town. Boutique hotel built in traditional style with elegant rooms and a tropical garden with pool. *99 rooms | 130 Minh Mang | approx. 3km (2mi) towards the Imperial tombs | tel. 054 3 88 54 61 | www.pilgrimagevillage.com | Expensive*

SAIGON MORIN

A colonial ambience, for connoisseurs. Magnificent breakfast in a pretty inner courtyard. Spacious rooms, attractively furnished; pool. *180 rooms | 30 Le Loi | tel. 054 3 82 35 26 | www.morinhotel. com.vn | Moderate–Expensive*

INFORMATION

Vietnam Tourism | 14 Nguyen Van Cu | tel. 054 3 82 83 16 | www.huefestival.com

WHERE TO GO

INSIDER TIP ▶ **BACH MA NATIONAL PARK** (135 D–E3) *(ﬂ G7)*

Situated some 40km (25mi) south of Hue, this national park covers some 220 sq km (85 sq mi) of mountainous terrain, cloaked in dense rainforest. It supports a rich variety of fauna, including a species of antelope, the saola (the giant muntjac), which was originally thought to be extinct but then rediscovered here in 1992. The rain-soaked park, which was only opened to the public a few years ago, is approached from the east by turning off the N 1 near the village of Cau Hai. From there it's just 16km (10mi) to the park's highest point, the 1444-m (4740-ft) Mount Bach Ma, which has magnificent views back to the sea. *Morin Bach Ma Hotel (12 rooms | tel. 054 3 87 11 99 | Budget)* is a rustic-style hotel with balcony rooms, a night club and restaurant. Please note usually full and very noisy at weekends. For information on accommodation in six basic guesthouses: *Tel. 054 3 87 13 30 | Budget. Park March–Sept 7am–5pm, Oct–Feb. 7.30am–4.30pm | www.bachma.vnn.vn | admission 20,000 dong*

CHUA THIEN MU (135 D3) *(ﬂ G7)*

A legend has grown up around the Heavenly Lady Pagoda (5km/3mi west of the city on the northern bank of the Perfume River). It is said that in 1601 the figure of an elderly lady appeared on a hill before the founder of the Nguyen dynasty, Nguyen Hoang. She insisted that this place belonged to a deity and demanded that for the prosperity of the nation a pagoda be built here. Nguyen Hoang obeyed her request – and the country and the Nguyen family prospered for hundreds of years.

In 1844 Emperor Thieu Tri added the octagonal, 21-m (70-ft) high *Phuoc Duyen tower*. Buddha statues are distributed across seven levels, with each level dedicated to a manushi-buddha (a Buddha in human form). The tower has become a symbol for Hue. A monk by the name of Thich Quang Duc, who practised in Thien Mu, caused a stir in 1963. He drove a light blue Austin car, now occupying a building to the rear of the pagoda, to Saigon and in protest at the cruelty of the Diem regime set himself on fire before the world's press.

LOW BUDGET

▶ Imagine you're staying in a museum – the Minh A *(Ancient Lodging House)* in Hoi An has five basic guest rooms in an almost 200-year-old timber house. No. 3 with a balcony overlooking the inner courtyard and its own bathroom is quieter than the street-side rooms (in some cases no windows, so not for tall people). Price for one night approx. 200,000 dong. *2 Nguyen Thai Hoc (by the market) | tel. 0510 3 86 13 68 | mobile 09 03 58 36 71*

▶ One unbeatable bargain in Hue is the *Binh Duong IV*. Ten rooms, with TV, PC, free WLAN, some with balconies, breakfast in bed or on the terrace, rooms from 275,000 dong. *7/25 Hai Ba Trung | tel. 054 3 84 96 62 | www.binhduonghotel.com*

▶ You can hardly miss the *Bun Bo Hue* restaurants *(e.g. 11 B Ly Thuong Kiet | tel. 054 3 82 64 60)*. The name says it all – you eat what arrives on the table. A bowl of *bun bo hue* is typically a Hue-style beef and rice noodle soup (approx. 20,000 dong).

ROYAL TOMBS (135 D3) (*M G7*)

The six royal tombs of the Nguyen dynasty are scattered across the countryside between 7km and 14km (4mi and 9mi) south of Hue. Many organised tours include the tombs in their itinerary, so, to avoid the crowds, it is better to arrange your own tour in a hired boat along the Perfume River (2 hours, including the Thien Mu Pagoda and Tomb of Minh Mang, approx. 30,000 dong), possibly including a taxi. As the tombs are some distance apart, hire a private boat and put a cycle on board. It only costs approx. 30,000 dong per day to hire one and you will find cycle hire outlets everywhere. But do check that the brakes are working properly. The immediate vicinity of the tombs can get very crowded, so try to make your visit early in the morning or early evening.

All the tombs were built to a similar pattern. Most of them are enclosed by a wall and are lined an honour courtyard with stone elephants, horses and civil and military mandarins. Each one has a stele pavilion in which the achievements of the deceased emperor are engraved on a marble tablet. Behind the pavilion is a temple for worshipping the Imperial family and then there's the mausoleum with the emperor's remains.

The Tomb of *Tu Duc* was built in 1848 by 3,000 forced labourers. It is situated 7km (4mi) from Hue and is surrounded by a wall and pond full of water lilies and lotus plants. Tu Duc's mausoleum, designed by the emperor himself, must be one of the most elegant and romantic tombs in Vietnam. He spent a lot of time here, devoting hours to poetry, chess and fishing. At the point where the two rivers, the Ta Trach and the Huu Trach merge to form the Perfume River, some 12km (7mi) from Hue, is the splendid Tomb of Emperor *Minh Mang*. Work started on it after his death in 1841. The palace, the pavilion and three magnificent gateways were built in a park around two large lakes, evoking a sense of space and peace.

Emperor *Khai Dinh's* tomb was built on Mount Chau between 1920 and 1931. Look carefully and you will see a fusion of Asian and European decorative features, testament to the emperor's inter-

19th century pavilion with the burial stele for Emperor Tu Duc

est in European culture. The multi-colour ceramic mosaics inside the temple add to the beauty and grace of this tomb. Khai Dinh, the twelfth emperor in the Nguyen dynasty, was the father of Emperor Bao Dai, the last Vietnamese ruler. The tombs of *Gia Long, Thieu Tri* and *Dong Khanh* are smaller and more modest.

Daily 7am–5pm | admission to each tomb approx. 55,000 dong. Always check your change.

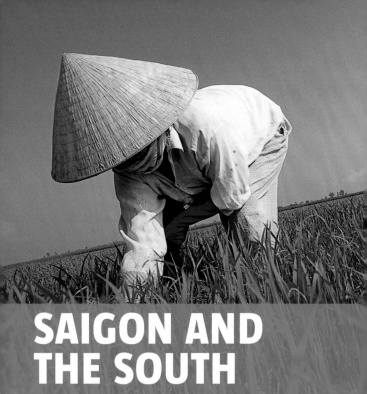

SAIGON AND THE SOUTH

Early in the morning is best, just after six o'clock, as the sun rises above the haze of the river delta – the Mekong, the vital artery of the south, where the nine arms or 'nine dragons' flow into the sea.
Vietnam is waking up as the boat's engine chugs on – fishermen in Chau Doc feed the catfish in the fish farms, in tiny restaurants men chat over their morning soup and tea or fragrant *ca phe*. Meanwhile, in the Can Tho rice noodle factory, the diesel-powered mixers rotate at full speed. On Cai Rang market, not just fruit and vegetables, but also cable and incense sticks, change hands – from boat to boat. Down here, on the Mekong, life is a long river.

Interestingly, here in the bustling Mekong delta, there always used to be fewer roadside posters with socialist party slogans – in contrast to the once hard-line communist north. 'Capitalist' ways could never disappear here. In the end, though, it's a fact: Hanoi is a long way off. Now Saigon and the surrounding region is the engine behind a second, quiet, but very visible revolution. It's happening in the urban smart-set, among a small, wealthy upper strata. But also in the rapidly growing middle class, which toils away industriously day and night. At first sight Saigon today is like a wasps' nest. Constantly on the move, unsettling and at the same time exhilarating.

If you're relaxing on the powder-white beaches of Nha Trang, Phan Thiet/Mui Ne or on Phu Quoc island, then it would be easy to imagine you were in the Carib-

Photo: Phan Thiet, women harvesting rice

The land of a thousand waterways – the Mekong Delta is Vietnam's rice bowl and there's an incessant hum of activity

bean, so stunningly beautiful are the holiday havens with their beautiful beaches, shady coconut palms and a crystal-clear sea. Laissez-faire and a typically tropical magic – that is the south of Vietnam.

CAN THO

(136 C4) (*E13*) **Long-tail boats, so called because of the outboard motor with an elongated propeller, which sweeps through the water like a whisk,** **shuttle back and forth along the countless canals and meandering waterways.** The boatmen navigate their wooden craft with extraordinary skill often along very narrow channels – but their homes and stilt houses are a long way from the main river. If you would like to explore the Mekong Delta off the beaten track, then you would be well advised to find accommodation in one of the hotels in this half-million strong city, which forms the political, commercial and cultural centre of the delta.

SIGHTSEEING

CAI RANG FLOATING MARKET ★ ●

Cai Rang market in Can Tho is the most vibrant and also the most attractive of the so-called 'floating markets' in the Mekong Delta. Every morning, countless

FOOD & DRINK

SAO HOM

A restaurant popular just as much with the Vietnamese as with the tourists. It's at a nice spot by the river, and is nearly always full. Huge selection of seafood,

Stall at Cai Rang floating market

rowing boats or long-tail boats heavily laden with melons and pineapples, cucumbers and soup saucepans congregate near the Da Sau bridge (approx. 6km/4mi from the city centre).

It's enthralling to watch the lively market scene – if you want to watch the whole spectacle from the water, then hire a boat from the centre of Can Tho near the market *(approx. 150,000 to 200,000 dong for 2 hours)*. It all gets going at sunrise and goes on until about 8am; by 9am activity is starting to tail off.

Chinese, Indian and Vietnamese classics such as spring rolls and hot pots, some Western (French) dishes and an excellent ice-cream menu. If it's just too crowded for you, then there are a number of inexpensive food stalls on the banks of the river. *50 Hai Ba Trung (Ninh Khieu pier on the promenade near the night market) | tel. 0710 3 81 56 16 | saohom.trans mekong.com | Moderate*

ENTERTAINMENT

How about *a trip on the Hau Giang river*? The traditional boats, which would resonate with (Chinese) opera arias and heart-breaking love songs *(don ca tai tu)*, left from Ninh Kieu Park promenade; they still moor there, but have been replaced by noisy three- or four-storey restaurant and disco vessels, adorned with strings of flashing lights. But perhaps – like the Vietnamese – you enjoy this brash and garish nightlife. It's a bit of Las Vegas in the Mekong Delta. Boats leave daily at 6pm and 8pm.

XE CLUB LOI (CYCLO CLUB)

If the crowded restaurant boats by the pier with their loud engines don't appeal to you, you can escape into this popular garden bar, and chill alongside groups of young Vietnamese. Live bands often play in the rustic-style western bar, or else a DJ takes charge. *Hau Giang Promenade (Hau riverside)*

WHERE TO STAY

KIM THO HOTEL

Take a ⚜ INSIDER TIPP▶ room on the 8th floor or higher of this modern hotel and you will get the added bonus of a fine view. It's a riverside hotel and so can be a little noisy, but the smart parquet floors, large bathrooms and elegant roof bar more than compensate. *51 rooms | 1 A Ngo Gia Tu | tel. 0710 3 81 75 17 | www. kimtho.com | Moderate*

VICTORIA CAN THO HOTEL

Even if you're not staying at the hotel, you can still treat yourself to a sundowner on the ⚜ terrace. You get superb views of the bustling activity on the river or the tropical garden in this colonial-inspired hotel. Plenty of recreational options and a *children's corner. 92 rooms | Cai Khe peninsula | tel. 0710 3 81 01 11 | www.victoriahotels-asia.com | Expensive*

INFORMATION

Can Tho Tourist | 20 Hai Ba Trung | tel. 0710 3 82 18 52 | www.canthotourist.info

---

⭐ **Cai Rang floating market**
Doing business on water – in Can Tho
→ p. 78

⭐ **Cho Lon**
Vibrant Chinatown in Saigon → p. 82

⭐ **Cao Dai Temple**
Multi-colour architecture in Tay Ninh → p. 91

⭐ **Chua Ngoc Hoang**
Heaven and hell in close proximity in Saigon's main temple → p. 82

⭐ **Boat trip on the Mekong Delta**
Take a tour on the mighty river – you can't leave Vietnam without a meander through the delta → p. 91

⭐ **History Museum**
Track down some of Vietnam's long forgotten civilisations in Saigon → p. 83

⭐ **Mui Ne**
A paradise for beach walkers and surfers → p. 96

⭐ **Nha Trang**
Beach resort and tourist hang-out – a fusion of Nice and Ibiza by the South China Sea → p. 92

⭐ **Phu Quoc**
If your dream is an inexpensive bungalow by the beach and ocean sunsets, then this is just the spot → p. 98

MARCO POLO HIGHLIGHTS

CHAU DOC

(136 B4) *(m D12)* **Everyday life in this city by the Cambodia border (pop. 100,000) still proceeds at a leisurely pace.**

Long-tail boats chug sedately along the Hau Giang river, children jump into the water from the decks of house boats, which float on empty oil drums. Many houseboats have nets slung beneath them, in which hundreds of thousands of catfish are farmed. The catch is then transported off to small fish-processing factories in Chau Doc, where they are dissected, deep frozen and exported all over the world. The city is also an important centre for the Vietnamese silk industry. Chau Doc is a melting pot of cultures, because in addition to the Moslem Cham, there are also many Chinese and Khmer.

INSIDER TIPP High-speed boats shuttle across the border from the Mekong Delta to Cambodia. Early each morning express boats belonging to *Blue Cruiser (www.bluecruiser.com | approx. 55US$, about 1,000,000 dong)* leave for Phnom Penh (returning later). The *Hang Chau express boats* and the *Tu Trang speedboat (www.tutrangtravel.com)* are slightly cheaper. The most exclusive way to make the journey is on the *Victoria Sprite*, but only guests of the Victoria Hotel *(www.victoriahotels-asia.com) may use it. All journey times approx. 4 hrs | Visa for Cambodia 20US$.*

SIGHTSEEING

CHAU GIANG

Cross the river either by ferry or private boat and you will reach the Cham village of Chau Giang. At the landing stage you are likely to be given a warm welcome by the Cham weavers. They are keen to tell visitors about their centuries-old weaving skills and also to sell, at very affordable prices, their INSIDER TIPP tasteful, delicately-patterned wraparound skirts. After a short walk through the village, you will reach the Chau Giang mosque, hard to miss given its conspicuous dome and tower. There's a great view over the town and the river from the ☀ tower. *Ferries leave from Chau Chiang jetty in Chau Doc about every 5–15 minutes*

NUI SAM ☀

The panoramic view from this 230-m (750-ft) mini-mountain some 3km (2mi) outside the town takes in the surrounding hills, rice fields and the region close to the Cambodian border. At sunset an air of mystery surrounds the many small temples and pagodas. Taoists, followers of Cao Dai, Christians, even Buddhists and Moslems, flock to Nui Sam Mountain in their thousands for the midnight festivities at New Year and also the annual Via Ba festival (May/June).

FOOD & DRINK

LAM HUNG KY

A restaurant for the locals near the market. Vietnamese and Chinese cuisine. *71 Chi Lang | 076 3 86 67 45 | Budget*

MEKONG

Dine out on classic Vietnamese dishes in the courtyard of a colonial villa. *41 Le Loi | opposite the Victoria Hotel | 076 3 86 73 81 | Moderate*

WHERE TO STAY

VICTORIA HOTEL ☀

This high-class hotel can offer delightful rooms with river view from stone balconies, plus amazing Vietnamese-French

Pedestrians, cycles, mopeds – traffic chaos in Saigon

cuisine. *93 rooms | 32 Le Loi | tel. 076 3 86 50 10 | www.victoriahotels-asia.com |* Expensive

Mekong Tours | 14 Nguyen Huu Canh | tel. 076 3 86 82 22 | www.mekongvietnam. com | www.hotels-chaudoc.com

HO CHI MINH CITY (SAIGON)

MAP INSIDE THE BACK COVER
(136 C3) (*E–F12*) **Saigon, with a population of around 6 million, is the old and the new power base for the Republic of Vietnam.**
While Hanoi can look back on a 1,000-year history, not yet 350 years have passed since, in 1674, the Vietnamese people started out on a long trek south, before settling in the place now officially

called Ho Chi Minh City (often shortened to HCMC).
Vietnam's largest city, divided into 19 districts *(quan),* has successfully retained much of its charm from the French colonial period. But this is how the Saigon of today looks: a vibrant metropolis, city of many millions of mopeds. Rickshaws and pedestrians fight for space between trucks and buses – the result is generally a noisy and chaotic free-for-all. But right in the middle of it all you will find colour-

CITY WHERE TO START?
Get a moped taxi, cyclo or taxi to **Notre Dame Cathedral**, where you can start your walk. Situated on Dong Khoi shopping boulevard (Rue Catinat in colonial days) are the classic hotels, such as the Continental or the Majestic. Carry on past the colonial General Post Office, the old Opera House and smart cafés as far as the river promenade. You can do it all on foot.

ful temples and pagodas and also markets such as *Binh Tay* in Saigon's 'Chinatown', the western district of ⭐ *Cho Lon.* Cho Lon used to be a separate settlement, its name means 'big market'. Refugees from southern China settled here about 300 years ago and started trading, and that is precisely what their descendants still do – on the pavements, in the narrow alleys and in the multi-storey mar-

Saigon Concert Hall. *Dong Khoi/corner of Le Loi corner | performances listed at hanoigrapevine.com*

CHUA GIAC LAM (0) (🗺 0)

Giac Lam Pagoda, the oldest in Saigon, was built in 1744. Ten monks live in the building, which reflects Taoist and Confucian influences. The most striking features are the 118 gilded wooden statues

Chua Ngoc Hoang – the faithful praying before the Buddha statue in the Jade Emperor Pagoda

ket hall. A ● journey by cyclo, a bicycle rickshaw, is an experience. Somehow your 'driver' manages to negotiate what most Europeans would regard as traffic mayhem.

SIGHTSEEING

OLD OPERA HOUSE/CITY THEATRE
(U E3) (🗺 e3)

The building, which dates from the start of the 20th century, was used post-1956 as an assembly hall for part of the South Vietnamese parliament. In 1975, it was re-opened as a theatre, and renamed

(including various portrayals of Buddha), the ornate carvings on the altar and on the 98 pillars in the main hall. *118 Lac Long Quan | 3km (2mi) northwest of Cho Lon*

CHUA NGOC HOANG ⭐ ●
(U D1) (🗺 d1)

In Saigon's main pagoda, the Taoists worship Ngoc Hoang, the powerful Jade Emperor. The main entrance flanked by guardian figures, however, leads first to a Buddhist altar with bodhisattiva images and the tam phat Buddha trinity. Only then do you arrive in the main hall with the statue of the Jade Emperor, surrounded by his ministers Bac Dau and Nam Tao, plus four guardians. The Chief of Hell, Thanh Hoang, dominates the side room to the left of the altar; the Torments of the Ten Hells are shown on wooden panels. But heaven is not far away. The small, usually smoke-filled room on the right attracts many parents and childless couples. Here twelve celestial women clad in precious silk give support to women hoping to conceive. Each ceramic figure (with children in arms) represents one year in the 12-year Chinese lunar calendar. *73 Mai Thi Luu | north of the city centre*

CHUA QUAN AM (0) *(M 0)*

The Fujian community built this pagoda in 1816, dedicating it to Quan Am, the Goddess of Mercy. It is regarded as one of the most beautiful in Cho Lon. On the first main altar you will see Thien Hau, revered as the Holy Mother Celestial Empress and Lady of the Sea, with Thich Ca, the historical Buddha (Sakyamuni), alongside her. This refers to the historical figure of Buddha in India, Siddhartha Gautama, who is also the Buddha of the Present Moment. Smiling satisfyingly at his side is Di Lac, the Buddha of the Future. In the open courtyard, dressed in white is Quan Am, flanked by General Bao Cong, Thanh Hoang, King of Hell and Than Tai, God of Finance. *12 Lao Tu*

CHUA THIEN HAU (0) *(M 0)*

Legend has it that Thien Hau, the patron saint of fishermen and mariners, can travel everywhere by riding the oceans on a mat or sitting astride the clouds. The pagoda was built in the early 19th century to honour the goddess of the Cantonese community. Considered to be the finest pagoda in Cho Lon, it is particularly admired for its magnificent ceilings adorned with intricate and colourful ceramic figures, among them a number of miniature demons. *710 Nguyen Trai/ corner of Trieu Quang Phuc | in the centre of Cho Lon*

GENERAL POST OFFICE (U D3) *(M d3)*

The striking features in the Main Post Office, built during the colonial era between 1886 and 1891, are the high-level cast-iron ceiling, lots of glass, the old maps, ceiling fans and chandeliers. But you may have other reasons to visit, e.g. to change money, make enquiries in the tourist information office or watch a water puppet theatre (shows daily 5pm and 6.30pm). *Dong Khoi (opposite the cathedral)*

HISTORY MUSEUM ★ (U E2) *(M e2)*

This fine building houses a variety of exhibits, which include a Bronze Age drum from the Dong Son dynasty. Particularly noteworthy are rooms no. 6 with ceramics from the Le Dynasty, nos. 7 and no. 8 with model boats, garments and instruments from the Tay Son dynasty, and no. 9 with ceramic vases from various Asian countries. In no. 12 is the Dong Duong bronze Buddha from the early Cham era. The museum also stages at least ten entertaining performances by the water *puppet theatre (9am, 10am, 11am, 2pm, 3pm and 4pm, ground floor room no. 11). Tue–Sun 8am–11am, 1.30pm–4.30pm | 2 Nguyen Binh Khiem | admission 15,000 dong | photography not permitted*

HO CHI MINH MUSEUM (BAO TANG HO CHI MINH) ● (U E4) *(M e4)*

The Nha Rong or Dragon House, built in 1863 at the point where the Ben Nghe canal joins the Saigon River, is where in 1911, a young communist named Ho Chi Minh, otherwise known as Ba, was hired as a kitchen boy for the Admiral Latouche

Tréville passenger steamer. Recalled in this interesting museum are this and other periods in the life of the great revolutionary. Do climb to the second floor to see the `INSIDER TIPP` pop art posters of Ho Chi Minh. *Tue–Sun 7.30am–11.30am, 1.30pm–5pm | 1 Nguyen Tat Thanh | admission 12,500 dong*

HÔTEL DE VILLE (U D3) (∅ d3)
The Hôtel de Ville, Saigon's town hall, was built between 1901 and 1908. Today it is the seat of Ho Chi Minh City's People's Committee. *At the northern end of Nguyen Hue*

A Christian church in Saigon – the Notre Dame Cathedral

NOTRE DAME CATHEDRAL (U D3) (∅ d3)
The cathedral stands at the northern end of Dong Khoi. This neo-Romanesque church built with reddish bricks dates from between 1877 and 1883. Two striking square towers topped by iron spires overlook the concourse. Mass is held every day at 4.30am and 5pm, Sun also at 9.30am.

WAR REMANTS MUSEUM (U C3) (∅ c3)
You may need strong nerves for this exhibition. Documented here in detail are the massacres committed by US forces during the Vietnam War on the Vietnamese population, notably in My Lai. Particularly chilling are the after-effects of chemical agents and dioxins. In the building's courtyard are captured tanks, helicopters and air defence weapons. If you would prefer to spare your children the sometimes rather disturbing images, you can leave them in the `INSIDER TIPP` play room on the second floor, where women will look after the little ones. *Daily 7.30am–noon, 1.30pm–5pm | 28 Vo Van Tan /corner of Le Qui Don | admission 15,000 dong*

ART MUSEUM (U D4) (∅ d4)
Formerly living quarters for CIA agents, this building is now used to showcase Vietnamese 20th century art. Exhibits in this renovated villa, which dates from the late 19th century, include statues in porcelain, clay and bronze, socialist realism paintings and items of designer furniture. *Tue–Sun 9am–5pm | 97 Duc Chinh | admission 15,000 dong*

REUNIFICATION PALACE (U D3) (∅ d3)
The Reunification Palace (Hoi Truong Thong Nhat) stands on the foundations of the Palais Norodom from 1862, at that time the seat of the French governor. In 1962, however, a South Vietnamese pilot

mounted an attack on the mansion with the intention of killing the hated President Ngo Dinh Diem. He survived the attempt, but the building was badly damaged.

Its replacement, which took four years to build, became known as South Vietnam's White House. But on 30 April 1975, before the world's press, it was stormed by North Vietnamese tanks. The finest room in the palace is the former audience room for ambassadors (2nd floor). There is a snack bar on the roof (4th floor). *Daily 7am-11am, 1pm–4pm | Visitors' entrance in Nam Ky Khoi Nghia | admission 15,000 dong*

FOOD & DRINK

You are sure to find somewhere INSIDER TIPP to suit your tastes on Nguy-en Dinh Chieu. Everything from small, down-to-earth Vietnamese snack bars to smart and spotless establishments, such as the *We* (near the War Remnants Museum / (U C3) (🗺 c3) | Budget–Moderate).

CHU BAR (U E3) (🗺 e3)

An interesting mix: during the day a nice coffee shop with snacks, such as noodle soups, in the evening an upmarket meeting place, where cigar smoke billows and fine wines are quaffed. *158 Dong Khoi | tel. 08 38 22 39 07 | Moderate*

INSIDER TIPP COM MINH DUC (U C4) (🗺 c4)

In this always crowded fast food outlet, with all the bustle of a station concourse, you pay according to the number of floral-patterned plastic plates you take. No menu, you simply select your traditional Vietnamese fare from the saucepans at the entrance. Loud and busy, but the food is very tasty. *Two restaurants: no. 35 and no. 100 Ton That Tung (northwest of the Pham Ngu Lao) | tel. 08 38 39 22 40 | Budget*

INSIDER TIPP CUC GACH QUAN
(U C1) (*M c1*)

In an old villa designed by architect Tran Binh, climb a narrow staircase to just below the roof. The dining area, like a rustic-style living room, has features ranging from the antique to the bizarre (e.g. a four-poster bed). But superb traditional cuisine is served here and with great attention to detail. Very popular with the locals. Reservation advisable. *10 Dang Tat | tel. 08 38 48 01 44 | www.cucgachquan.com.vn/en | Moderate*

LA HABANA (U E3) (*M e3*)
Tapas and mojitos, sangria and salsa, cigars and paella – a popular bar-restaurant with a distinctive Cuban ambience. Over 50 different tapas. *6 Cao Ba Quat | tel. 08 38 29 51 80 | www.lahabana-saigon.com | Moderate*

HIGHLANDS COFFEE
(U E3) (*M e3*)

After a mini-souvenir shopping spree *(on the 3rd floor)*, sit in the rooftop restaurant of this central department store and enjoy the view over the bustling scene below at the Nguyen Hue/Le Loi junction. Try a beef BBQ, prawns and a cooling beer *(daily 9am–11pm)*. To reach the roof terrace *(4th floor)*, climb the stairs at the rear of the 3rd floor restaurant. *135 Nguyen Hue | on the right next to the Kim Do Royal City Hotel | tel. 08 39 14 49 92 | www.highlandscoffee.com.vn | Budget–Moderate*

HOI AN (U E3) (*M e3*)
Dine out to the accompaniment of traditional Vietnamese music in this upmarket restaurant in a beautiful teak villa, spread over two floors. Duck in Hoi An style, seafood and fish, vegetarian dishes and menus from 450,000 dong. Popular with tour groups. Reservation advisable. *Only open in the evening from 5.30pm | 11 Le Thanh Ton | tel. 08 38 23 76 94 | Expensive*

QUAN AN NGON (NHA HANG NGON)
(U D3) (*M d3*)

Always a full house here for authentic Vietnamese cuisine. Sit outdoors or in the two-storey building. Be sure to try the delicious goi bo bop thau, a spicy beef salad with banana and slices of star fruit. *160 Pasteur | tel. 08 39 33 61 33 | Budget–Moderate*

INSIDER TIPP TEMPLE CLUB
(U E4) (*M e4*)

A staircase leads upstairs through the plain hallway to the villa. Excellent Vietnamese fare, such as grilled fish in banana leaf *(ca nuong la chuoi)* and sweet Hue cakes *(banh dau xanh hue)*. High ceiling exposed brick walls. Nice atmosphere in the lounge bar. *29–31 Ton That Thiep | tel. 08 38 29 92 44 | Moderate–Expensive*

WRAP & ROLL (U C4) (*M c4*)
A thousand and one variations on the spring roll in a modern snack bar chain. Choose with prawns or Hue style. Both always delicious. As well as breakfast, the menu lists salads, soups and desserts, fish and vegetarian dishes, hot pots in the evening. *97 B Nguyen Trai, also 111 Nguyen Hue | tel. 08 39 25 36 39 | www.wrap-roll.com | Budget*

Dong Khoi – recommended for your shopping expedition

SHOPPING

After a busy day sightseeing, a shopping spree in the boulevards of District 1 will be time well spent; choose between silk clothing, chopsticks and lacquerware in Dong Khoi *(rather expensive, e.g. at Vietsilk | no. 21)*, Hai Ba Trung and Le Loi *(all* (U D–E3) *(𝄞 d–e3))* or in the Nguyen Van Troi galleries. Armani and Gucci, a great food market, plus games rooms for the youngsters in the ● *Vincom Center (70 Le Thanh Ton |* (U E3) *(𝄞 e3))*. Antiques and dusty Buddhas in all shapes and sizes in Le Cong Kieu, the secondhand dealers' street *(try the Ngoc Bich family | no. 64 |* (U D4) *(𝄞 d4))*.

Cheap and cheerful imitations, DVDs, T-shirts and everything tourists need on their travels are available in the *Saigon Square department store (Ton Duc Thang |* (U E2) *(𝄞 e2))*. And also in the good old (inexpensive) *Thuong Xa Tax department store,* INSIDERTIPP you can haggle, e.g. for souvenirs on the 3rd floor *(Nguyen Hue near the Kim Do Hotel |* (U E3) *(𝄞 e3))*. Alternatively, barge through the crowds in the 100-year-old *Ben Thanh market* (U D4) *(𝄞 d4)* (souvenirs at the western entrance, do haggle, cash machine available). In the evening it becomes a night market with food stalls. Slightly cheaper are *Bin Tay Market* in Chinatown *(Cholon district, see p. 82)*, and the alleys lined with shops, food stalls and restaurants around the Pham Ngu Lao backpacker quarter (U C–D4) *(𝄞 c–d4)*.

INSIDERTIPP NGUYEN FRÈRES
(U E3) *(𝄞 e3)*

A well-stocked shop and a great place to browse. Crafts and weavings by the hill tribes, water puppets, Buddhas, bags, scarves, jewellery, ceramics and lacquerware, furniture and lamps. *Daily 9am–9pm | 2 Dong Khoi (near the Saigon River) | www.nguyenfreres.com*

SPORTS & ACTIVITIES

Trails of Indochina: Tours of Indochina. *10/8 Phan Dinh Giot (near the airport) | tel. 08 38 44 10 05 | www.trailsofindochina.com*

L'APOTHIQUAIRE DAY SPA ●
(U D3) (𝄞 d3)

One of the best day spas in town, near the Rex Hotel as well as in an old villa (pick-up service). *Daily 9am–8pm | Le Thanh Ton 64 A | Truong Dinh | tel. 08 39 32 51 81 | www.lapothiquaire.com*

GOLF

Vietnam Golf & Country Club: 36-hole course 15km (9mi) east of the city centre. Green fee on weekdays from approx. 1,000,000 dong, practice round approx. 300,000 dong. Also tennis. *Long Thanh My Ward/Village | (0) | tel. 08 62 80 01 01 | www.vietnamgolfcc.com*

ENTERTAINMENT

INSIDER TIPP CA PHE THU BAY ●
(U D2) (𝄞 d2)

If you enjoy mingling with the locals, then you will be at ease in this romantic garden café. Only beer, soft drinks, coffee, tea, yogurt, ice cream, pasta dishes, plus a few other snacks (*Budget*). *Daily 7am–11pm | 37 Nguyen Dinh Chieu*

INSIDER TIPP CARMEN BAR
(U E3) (𝄞 e3)

Live bands, predominantly Latino and Flamenco sounds in this dimly-lit setting, plus cocktails, beer, wine, whisky. Packed to the rafters at weekends. *Daily 7pm–midnight | 8 Ly Tu Trong*

LUSH (U E2) (𝄞 e2)

Popular club disco, crowded at weekends from 11pm (House: Mon, Sat; Pop/ house: Wed, Sun; Latin/house: Thu). Chill out in the relatively quiet courtyard by the bar. *2 Ly Tu Trong*

Q BAR (U E3) (𝄞 e2)

A veritable hot spot. The interior is a mix of Art Deco, vaulted cellar, Mediterranean hotel and postmodern style. *Daily 6pm–midnight | 7 Lam Son | opposite the Caravelle Hotel | www.qbarsaigon.com*

SAX 'N' ART CLUB (U D3) (𝄞 d3)

Small and friendly jazz club run by saxophonist Tran Manh Tuan. Large screen and jazz videos to watch while sipping cocktails, until the live bands get started from 9pm. Happy Hour 5pm–8pm. *Daily 5pm–midnight | 28 Le Loi*

MUNICIPAL THEATRE (U E3) (𝄞 e3)

Gymnastics performances in massed ranks, high-quality Vietnamese theatre, classical music, ballet and rock/ pop concerts. *Daily 8pm | Dong Khoi/corner of Le Loi corner | tel. 08 38 29 99 76 and 38 25 15 63 | listings on hanoigrapevine. com | tickets from 80,000 dong*

WATER PUPPET THEATRE
(U D3) (𝄞 d3)

The *Rong Vang Golden Dragon Water Puppet Theatre* is a fine example of the genre, 200 seats *(performances daily 5pm and 6.30pm | 55 B Nguyen Thi Minh Khai | tel. 08 39 30 21 96 | admission 100,000 dong).* Water puppet theatre also during the day in the History Museum *(see p. 83).*

WHERE TO STAY

In *Pham Ngu Lao* street (U C–D4) (𝄞 c–d4) (pronounced something like 'farm mu lao'), a district with guest houses, cafes and bars, travel agencies, banks, tailors and souvenir shops etc. has evolved. There really is nowhere else in the country where you will find such good and, at the same time, inexpensive accommodation as here. The mini-hotels are almost all of good quality. On the new park site known as *'23.9.'* (U C–D4) (𝄞 c–d4) off Le Lai street, you can join in with the jogging, tai chi and gymnastics. There's an early start, usually around 5.30am. The central *Thi Sach street* in District 1 has seen a lot of new hotels open, many of which are in the mid-range, business category, i.e. the *May Hotel* with a covered rooftop pool (*118 rooms | 28–30 Thich Sach | (U E3) (□ e3) | tel. 08 38 23 45 01 | www. mayhotel.com.vn | Moderate*).

CONTINENTAL HOTEL ●
(U E3) (□ e3)
Evidence of the big wide world outside Vietnam, and a more leisurely era, can be found in Saigon's oldest hotel, which dates from 1885. Famous literary figures, such as Somerset Maugham and Graham Greene, stayed in this grand hotel, which was the backdrop for much of the latter's Quiet American. Pretty courtyard. *87 rooms | 132–134 Dong Khoi | tel. 08 38 29 92 01 | www.continentalvietnam.com | Expensive*

DUXTON (U E4) (□ e4)
Four-star hotel in the heart of the city, rooms on the upper floors are the quietest; giant buffet breakfast, small pool, nice piano bar in the lobby. One negative: no Wi-Fi. *198 rooms | 63 Nguyen Hue | tel. 08 38 22 29 99 | www.duxtonhotels.com | Expensive*

HAPPY INN (U C4) (□ c4)
Friendly guest house in the travellers' quarter; with lift. Rooms of different sizes with IDD, TV, Wi-Fi, refrigerator, some with balcony. INSIDER TIPP Room no. 71, the VIP Balcony Room, is highly sought-after: quiet with roof terrace and pot plants (*Moderate*). *19 rooms | 178 Bui Vien (near Pham Ngu Lao) | tel. 08 38 38 53 37 | www. happy-inn.net | Budget–Moderate*

The City Theatre has been back in use for evening events since 1975

HO SEN HOTEL (U E3) (⌘ e3)

The small, centrally located Lotus Lake hotel can offer comfortable rooms on seven floors with lift, satellite TV, some with river view. Small restaurant. *45 rooms | 4 B–4 C Thi Sach | tel. 08 38 23 22 81 | www.hosenhotel.com.vn | Budget–Moderate*

KIM DO ROYAL CITY HOTEL (U E3) (⌘ e3)

Creative mix of Asian rattan armchairs, mahogany furniture and formal Japanese teak design. Book over the Internet and get a discount of up to 40 percent. *132 rooms | 133 Nguyen Hue | tel. 08 38 22 59 14 | www.kimdohotel.com | Moderate–Expensive*

MADAM CUC MINIHOTELS (U C5) (⌘ c5)

Basic, tiled rooms with bathroom, some with balcony (quieter at rear), satellite TV, refrigerator, air-conditioning. Inclusive deal of two meals, coffee, tea, juice and fruit at any time, airport pickup and tour information. There are two more Madam Cuc hotels in the same street (nos. 64 and 184). *20 rooms | 127 Cong Quynh | tel. 08 38 36 87 61 | www.madamcuchotels.com | Budget*

THIEN XUAN HOTEL (U D4) (⌘ d4)

Nice rooms, stucco ceilings, some with balcony (rooms at front noisy), friendly and professional service. *60 rooms | 108–110 Le Thanh Ton (near Ben Thanh Market) | tel. 08 38 24 56 80 | www.thienxuanhotel.com.vn | Moderate*

INFORMATION

Tourist information in the General Post Office (Dong Khoi | opposite the cathedral)

WHERE TO GO

INSIDER TIPP CAT TIEN NATIONAL PARK ☺ (137 D3) (⌘ F11)

The industrial area north of Saigon seems endless, but there's no avoiding it. First you're on the N 1, then on Provincial Road 20. After 150km (90mi) you will arrive at the gates of the tropical Cat Tien National Park. The park boasts swamps, savannah, mountains and lowland plains, so scenically it is very varied. Now a Unesco Biosphere Reserve, it's definitely worth exploring. The World Wildlife Fund also has a hand in its management, as it is one of the last refuges of the Indochinese tiger. Unfortunately WWF and Unesco stewardship could not save the Javan rhinoceros. Until 2010 one of two populations in the wild was surviving here, but that is now thought to be extinct. But leopards and rare animals, such as the gaur (Indian bison), are safe.

Some 360 bird species have been counted in the park, so it is a favourite haunt for ornithologists. If you decide to go on an exploratory tour, you have to be accompanied by a guide, for which a charge of about 300,000 dong is made. Basic overnight accommodation (*Budget*) is available at the park entrance. Further information from the *National Park Service (tel. 061 3 66 92 28 | www.namcattien.org | admission approx.60,000 dong)*.

CU CHI ● (136 C3) (⌘ F12)

The moment you arrive at this complex of tunnels you will be reminded of the horrors of war. At the entrance to the Cu Chi Tunnels in the village *Ben Dinh* (approx. 60km/40mi west of Saigon), you will see the gun of a rusty tank taking aim, beside it a military helicopter. The visitors' entrance leads into a 50-m (160-ft) long restored section of cool and damp tunnel, which, despite widening, is still quite narrow. These underground galleries, formerly controlled by the Viet Cong, once extended for 250km (150mi), covering an area of about 400sq km (150sq mi). They were equipped with canteens, hospitals and rest rooms – all up to 10m (30ft) below ground. The tunnels were so narrow that only the Vietnamese could squeeze through. Women were often brought underground to give birth in safety; mother and child were then able to stay there for weeks.

Now countless souvenir stalls are clustered around the tunnel entrance area; there's even a shooting range if you need to while away some time. An open-air museum and a war memorial remember the military action and those that died. *On the N 22 to Tay Ninh | www.cuchi tunnel.org.vn | admission 100,000 dong*

MY THO (136 C4) (*F12*)

The first busy spot on the road out to the Mekong Delta is the provincial capital of My Tho (pop. 180,000), about 70km (40mi) south of Saigon and a two-hour drive through fertile rice paddies. This is a good place to start a ⭐ *boat tour of the Mekong Delta*. You will find yourself inundated with offers from vociferous freelance boat owners, as you pass along the riverside road, *30 Thang 4*, not far from the tourist information office. The long-tail boats with their rattling engines and long propeller shafts often have to squeeze through tiny channels on their way past tiny temples, busy markets, coconut groves and banana plantations. Possible destinations are the *floating market of Cai Be*, the islands of *Con Phung* (Island of the Coconut Monk) or *Thoi Son*. Be prepared to negotiate a price. Don't pay more than 200,000 dong per boat for a 2-hour tour. *Information: Chuong Duong Tourist | no. 8 in 30*

Thang 4 street | tel. 073 3 87 31 84 and 3 87 34 77

TAY NINH (136 C3) (*E12*)

Tay Ninh (pop. 42,000), 95km (60mi) west of Saigon, is the capital of the eponymous province and since 1927 the centre of the Cao Dai religion. Many are inclined to dismiss Caodaiism as a rather contradictory fusion, but the town is defi-

A fusion of cathedral and mosque – the Cao Dai Temple in Tay Ninh

nitely worth a visit, if only to admire the extraordinary architecture of the ⭐ *Cao Dai Temple*. It can be found in the village of Long Hoa, about 4km (3mi) east of the city centre, on a spacious concourse (the 'Holy See'), which can hold up to 100,000 faithful followers. The temple itself is a mixture of a twin-tower cathedral, a pagoda with round tower and a mosque with a domed roof. The striking features inside are the deep blue sky with stars made from mirror glass, the pillars entwined with dragons and the 'divine eyes'. The prayer ceremony is held four times a day – at 6am, noon, 6pm and at midnight. Tourists must watch from the upstairs balcony. Ceremonies in the morning can get very crowded, so it is advisable to attend the evening or midnight prayer session.

If you have time, consult the map and make for the 1,000m (3,250ft) ☾ *Nui Ba Den* (Mountain of the Black Woman) volcanic cone, approx. 15km (10mi) northeast of the city centre. Once a holy shrine for the Khmer and still a place of pilgrimage, there is a stunning view from the summit.

Information/accommodation: *Tay Ninh Tourist (tel. 066 3 82 23 76)* runs a small office in the basic *Hoa Binh Hotel (97 rooms | no. 210 in 30 Thang 4 street | tel. 066 3 82 13 15 | www.viehotel.com/ hoabinhhotel | Budget)*.

NHA TRANG

(137 F2) *(㏝ H11)* ⭐ **The picturesque coastal town of Nha Trang (pop. 300,000) has grown into a busy tourist centre, a Vietnamese-style fusion of Nice and Ibiza.**

The real attraction of Nha Trang, though, is its geographical location. Situated in a broad bay on the South China Sea, the city is bordered to the north by towering Hon Son mountain range. Offshore are a number of small green islands, which look the perfect place for dreamy afternoons lounging beneath palm trees. The Tran Phu waterfront seems to go on forever, in fact it follows the beach for more than 5km (3mi). It ends in the south at the idyllic fishing harbour of Cau Da.

SIGHTSEEING

LONG SON PAGODA ☾

A chua built in honour of Kim Than Phat, the white Buddha, who sits in a highly

A garden for Buddha – Long Son Pagoda in Nha Trang

visible position to its rear. Some 152 stone steps lead up from Long Son, past a huge reclining Buddha. The pagoda itself was built in the late 19th century. Look out for the brightly-coloured dragons wrapped around the pillars either side of the main altar. *Thai Nguyen, approx. 500m west of the station*

PO NAGAR ☼

The Po Nagar Cham temple on a hill in the north of town has become a symbol for Nha Trang. Consisting of four towers, it was probably built between the 9th and 13th century. It is dedicated to Po Ino Nagar, the goddess who watches over the city and an incarnation of Shiva. From the pagoda complex, there is a fine view over the harbour and its brightly painted fishing boats. *Daily 6am–6pm | admission 5,000 dong*

FOOD & DRINK

INSIDER TIPP ▶ **NGOC SUONG**

Friendly restaurant with tables outdoors. Guests are treated to very good service, excellent fish and great value for money. *96 Tran Phu | promenade near Phu Dong Water Park & night market | tel. 058 3 52 56 77 | www.ngocsuong.com.vn | Moderate–Expensive*

SAILING CLUB – SANDALS RESTAURANT

Dimly-lit garden and beach restaurant, but also a popular disco club. From 10pm onwards, it's crowded, loud and hot (camp-fire). Crossover dishes with Japanese, Italian, Greek, Vietnamese and Indian influences, plus lots of cocktails. *72–74 Tran Phu | tel. 058 3 52 46 28 | www.sailingclubvietnam.com | Budget–Moderate*

The perfect place to relax – Nha Trang beach

LEISURE, SPORTS & BEACH

ISLAND TOURS

Boat tours to the offshore islands are very popular. When booking a tour, be cautious. Ask other travellers about their experiences with the various travel agencies. The following are considered to be reliable companies: *Jungle Travel (3 L Hung Vuong | www.vietnamjungletravel. com)* or *Nha Trang Adventures (also trekking, mountain biking, kayaking | www. adventures-nt.com).*

A cable car crosses the sea to *Hon Tre (daily 8am–10pm | approx. 80,000 dong)*

BEACH

The 6-km (4-mi) long *Nha Trang beach* is lined almost entirely with coconut palms. Hire a lounger and enjoy a relaxing day in the sun.

DIVING

Rainbow Divers is the leading diving operator in Vietnam and also offers courses in Nha Trang. *Rainbow Bar (90 A Hung Vuong | tel. 058 3 52 43 51) | Restaurant La Louisiane (Tran Phu Beach | tel. 058 3 52 19 48) | tel. for Whale Island 058 3 81 37 88 | 24 hr hotline / mobile 09 08 78 17 56 | www.divevietnam.com*

ENTERTAINMENT

Beach parties Ibiza-style are popular events. Someone somewhere lights a bonfire, then house music or a gentle lounge sound emanates from speakers and no-one goes to bed before sunrise. The action usually takes place near the spacious *Sailing Club* or *La Louisiane Brewhouse & Restaurant (Tran Phu Beach | Lot 29, Tran Phu | tel. 058 3 52 19 48 | www.louisianebrewhouse.com.vn),* both open approx. 11pm–5am. Great view over the bay from the ☼ roof terrace during 'happy hour' *(6pm–10pm)* at *Jack's Bar (96 A/8 Tran Phu | tel. 058 3 81 38 62)*. Plus billiards.

WHERE TO STAY

ASIA PARADISE HOTEL ☼

Modern, smart and bright rooms with parquet floors and all modern conveniences, some with huge window or balcony looking out to sea (8th–11th floor). Nice roof terrace restaurant, plus small pool, massage, sauna, fitness suite. *79 rooms | 6 Biet Thu | tel. 058 3 52 46 86 | www.asiaparadisehotel.com | Moderate–Expensive*

EVASON ANA MANDARA RESORT & SPA

This first-class beach hotel with 74 bungalows and villas (some with sea view) in a tropical garden exudes pure luxury. Painstaking attention to detail and beautiful bamboo-timber-rattan décor. Facilities include two open-air restaurants, pools and a tennis court, plus a wide choice of water sports. *86 Tran Phu | tel. 058 3 52 47 05 | www.sixsenses.com | Expensive*

INSIDER TIPP TIDE HOTEL

A trendsetting hot spot – away from all the tourist crowds, this simple mini-hotel is situated on the (noisy) beach road. There are rooms with sea view or you could go for a quieter, rear-facing room, all with satellite TV. At sunrise, you can sit on the balcony and watch (or join in with) the locals doing their tai chi exercises in the small bay at Hon Chong (or go and join in). A number of seafood restaurants nearby, the city centre is about 2km (1.25mi) away. *10 rooms | 1 A Pham Van Dong (Bai Duong) | tel. 058 3 83 69 51 | www.thetidehotel.com | Budget*

INFORMATION

Khanh Hoa Tourist | 1 Tran Hung Dao | tel. 058 3 52 67 53 | www.nhatrangtourist.com.vn

WHERE TO GO

If you crave tranquillity and solitude, then the idyllic *Doc Let Beach* on the *Hon Khoi* peninsula (137 F2) (*ID H10*) about 50km (30mi) north of the city (fork off near Ninh Hoa) is thoroughly recommended. The INSIDER TIPP *Ki-em Art House Resort (Dong Hai, Ninh Hai, Ninh Hoa | tel. 058 3 67 09 52 | www.ki-em.com | Expensive)* is run by the artist,

Ki-em. The nine bungalows with poster beds, nice bathroom and terrace looking out to sea overlook a long, flat beach. There is even a meditation room with ancient pagoda columns. Also on the peninsula is a haven dedicated to pure luxury, the **INSIDER TIPP** *Evason Hideaway & Spa at Ana Mandara (52 villas | Ninh Van Bay, Ninh Hoa | tel. 058 3 72 82 22 || www.sixsenses.com | Expensive).*

sauce. But more importantly, Phan Thiet **boasts the delightful ⭐ Mui Ne peninsula and a wide sweeping bay beneath coconut palms, one reason why it has become one of Vietnam's most popular beach destinations.**

It was 1995 when the first beach bungalow resort opened here, now it competes against 200 hotels in the 3- to 4-star category along the 16km (10mi), in part

Oxen cooling down in Mui Ne fishing harbour

Rustic-style but very comfortable villas made from natural materials by the beach, on stilts above the water, tucked away among rocks or on a hill, all with a small pool. Accessible only by boat (approx. 20 minutes).

PHAN THIET

(137 E3) (∅ *G12*) **The provincial capital (pop. 170,000) is famous for its fish**

boulevard-style coast road.

Nevertheless, you will still see fishermen attending to their boats, nets and baskets on the beach – in some places it's very narrow. The long, sun-drenched coastline – with its varied landscape ranging from Sahara-style dunes to rain forests, plus the right sort of waves for surfing – attracts investors and tourists alike. However, subject to the season, wind and weather, the beach can get badly eroded and polluted.

A brick-red landscape – a walk along the Red Sand Canyon

PO SHANU TOWERS ☼

Near Mui Ne beach, on the *Ngoc Lam Hill*, stands Vietnam's southernmost Cham shrine. The three small Po Shanu towers, dating from the 8th-century, but restored in 1999, are less ornate than the famous towers of Po Nagar and Po Klong Garai; they were dedicated to the Queen Po Shanu. A beautiful panoramic view extends from here along the coast and over the town of Phan Thiet.

FOOD & DRINK

RUNG FOREST RESTAURANT

Large, jungle-effect restaurant with terracing on to the street. Mainly Vietnamese cuisine, but also pasta, wines and cocktails. Folkloric-themed performances in the evening. *67 Nguyen Dinh Chieu | tel. 062 3 84 75 89 | www.forestrestaurant. com | Budget–Moderate*

TRUNG DUONG

Simple beach restaurant with excellent fish dishes (try the red snapper). Western-style breakfasts, but also traditional Vietnamese fare, e.g. Vietnamese wine. *Near the Coco Beach Resort | km 13 marker | Ham Tien | tel. 062 3 84 74 20 | Budget*

SIGHTSEEING

MUI NE PENINSULA ★

The small town of *Mui Ne* has a lively harbour and some small fish sauce factories. Gleaming brightly at the end of the peninsula are the celebrated reddish-orange to yellowy-white dunes *(Bao Trang)*. You can get to the top in a jeep or you can walk, but not barefoot. By 9am, the sand is red hot! Close to Hon Nghe Bay is *Ba Bau* or White Lake, a picturesque lakeland area with lotus flowers surrounded by snow-white sand dunes.

SPORTS & ACTIVITIES

SURFING

Every February, hundreds of water sport enthusiasts meet up in Mui Ne for the *Fun Cup*. As Phan Thiet and Mui Ne are in what is considered to be a low rainfall region, the resorts attract an international band of surfers throughout almost the entire year. The best times for surfing are September/October to December, for kite surfing November to March/April. *www.windsurf-vietnam.com*

WALKING

One popular walk (it takes about one hour) starts near the village of *Ham Tien* and follows a stream through the dunes and past the bright red rock walls of the small *Red Sand Canyon* as far as the cascading source of the Suoi Tien *(Fairy Spring)*.

ENTERTAINMENT

JIBE'S

Where the surfers meet up in the evening – in the middle of the beach. *90 Nguyen Dinh Chieu | km 13 marker | www.windsurf-vietnam.com*

MIA MUI NE

Lifestyle club for the smart set with the excellent *Sandals Restaurant* (fusion food, *Moderate)*, plus upmarket ● beach bar serving great cocktails. *24 Nguyen Dinh Chieu | Ham Tien | www.sailingclubvietnam.com and www.miamuine.com*

POGO BAR

Relax in a hammock or lounge around on huge bean bags on the beach. Billiards, beach volleyball, pogo party by firelight. *138 Nguyen Dinh Chieu | km 16 marker | Ham Tien*

WHERE TO STAY

CHAM VILLAS

An excellent spot on the Mui Ne – stylishly-decorated bungalows with palm-leaf roofs, four poster beds, lush greenery, giant pool. *16 bungalows | 32 Nguyen Dinh Chieu | Ham Tien | tel. 062 3 74 12 34 | www.chamvillas.com | Expensive*

COCO BEACH RESORT

One of the nicest bungalow villages on the beach – stilt houses and villas dotted around by the beach and in the garden (no TV, but air-conditioned). Two very good restaurants, small pool. *34 bungalows | 58 Nguyen Dinh Chieu | km 12.5 marker | Ham Tien | tel. 062 3 84 71 11 | www.cocobeach.net | Moderate–Expensive*

INSIDER TIPP FULL MOON BEACH RESORT

Pretty, timber bungalows, rooms with four-poster beds and pink-tiled bathrooms. Where the surfing set stay. *27*

LOW BUDGET

▶ The *Lac Canh* in Nha Trang is a lively outdoor restaurant with a station concourse atmosphere. It gets crowded in the evening. Seafood (from 50,000 dong), chicken, BBQ beef (from 40,000 dong). *44 Nguyen Binh Khiem | Nha Trang, | tel. 058 3 82 13 91*

▶ *Jungle Beach Resort (Home Stay)*: Ultra-wide beach, spartan chalets (walls made from roller blinds, shared toilet facilities), approx. 1,000,000 dong, three vegetarian meals included. *Hon Khoi peninsula, some 60km (37mi) north of Nha Trang | tel. 058 3 62 23 84 | mobile 09 13 42 91 44 | www.junglebeachvietnam.com*

▶ *Cat Huy Hotel*: In the heart of Saigon's backpacker quarter at the end of a quiet street – a six-storey mini-hotel (no lift) with ten bright and cosy rooms (king-size beds, flat screen TV, minibar, some with balcony). From 500,000 dong. *10 rooms | 353/28 Pham Ngu Lao | tel. 08 39 20 87 16 | www.cathuyhotel.com*

rooms | km 13.5 marker | Ham Tien | tel. 062 3 84 70 08 | www.windsurf-vietnam. com | *Moderate*

HIEP HOA RESORT

Tightly-packed blue chalets and a two-storey building; the rows of chalets have fans or air conditioning and terrace or balcony overlooking the shady gardens or palm beach. A new nightclub has opened nearby. *15 rooms | 80 Nguyen Dinh Chieu | tel. 062 3 84 72 62 | www. muinebeach.net/hiephoa | Budget*

MIA RESORT

Pretty complex, rooms with French balconies, Australian management. *31 rooms | 24 Nguyen Dinh Chieu | Ham Tien | tel. 062 3 84 74 40 | www.sailingclubvietnam. com | Moderate–Expensive*

INFORMATION

Vidotour Travel | 65 Nguyen Dinh Chieu | tel. 062 3 84 76 99 | www.vidotourtravel. com | www.muinebeach.net

WHERE TO GO

TA CU ☆ (137 E3) (*ØJ G11*)

On the 58-m (190-ft) high Ta Cu (also known as Ta Ku) in the ☺ nature reserve of the same name is probably the tallest Buddha statue in Vietnam. The Sakyamuni Buddha measures a total of 49m (160ft) from the tips of his toes to the top of his enlightened head. To reach the statue involves either a 2-hour hike through the woods, or – more comfortably – a 10-minute cable-car ride. At the top pilgrims and visitors are warmly welcomed to the over 150-year-old *Linh Son Truong Tho* monastery. *Daily 6.30am–6pm | approx. 30km (20mi) southwest of Phan Thiet near Ham Thuan Nam | admission approx. 80,000 dong*

PHU QUOC

(136 A4) (*ØJ C–D 12–13*) ★ **Holiday where the black peppercorns grow – Vietnam's largest island is close to the Cambodian border.**

The plots for countless luxury resorts have already been earmarked (unfortunately currently many are still building sites). Awaiting development, mainly on the south coast, are some 40km (30mi) of beaches fringed with coconut palms against a jungle backdrop. Where propeller planes from Saigon now land, near the island's capital of Duong Dong, will in a few years time be an international airport welcoming visitors from all over Asia. Plans for four golf courses, a cruise-ship quay and a casino have been approved. Phu Quoc (pop. 90.000) is set to become Vietnam's answer to Thailand's Phuket, with an expected 2–3 million tourists per year.

In the winter season, every day there are nine flights to Phu Quoc from Saigon, five from Can Tho and one from Rach Gia, as well as several speed boats (approx. 275,000 dong) from Ha Tien and Rach Gia. Not recommended are the cheap ferries from Ba Hon/Ha Tien. They are

dangerous, especially during the rainy season, and may even be illegal.

SIGHTSEEING

NATIONAL PARK

Phu Quoc means '99 mountains'. However, the mountains in the north of the national park, which rise to 600m (1,950ft), are still part of a restricted military zone. On the rough track by the east and north coast tall trees provide welcome shade, while the crickets in the rainforest sound like a whistling kettle. If you make a tour around the national park and the island, at Phu Quoc's northwestern tip near the fishing village of *Ganh Dau*, you will see the coast of Cambodia and the island of *Ses* just 4km (2.5mi) away.

FOOD & DRINK

EDEN

A restaurant and guest house by the southern section of Bai Truong beach. From breakfast egg to cocktails, from billiards to disco dancing – all needs met from early morning until late at night. *118 Tran Hung Dao | 7 Ward (Beach Rd) | tel. 077 3 98 55 98 | www.edenresort. co.vn | Moderate*

MY LANH AND AI XIEM

Typical Vietnamese beach restaurants on Bai Sao, serving delicious seafood and fish. Accommodation available in some rather spartan chalets (but it is a lively spot at the weekend). *Budget*

SAKURA

Cook Kiem serves up delicious home-made food, always fresh too. Lots of seafood and fish dishes and excellent curries. *Access road to Ong Long beach (near Mango Bay Resort) | tel. 0773 98 51 37 | mobile 0122 8 18 34 84 | Budget*

TROPICANA RESORT

This well-known resort is almost always full, but then its idyllic terrace restaurant with bar beside Truong beach is hard to resist. Good seafood; Vietnamese and European dishes on the menu. *Bai Truong | tel. 077 3 84 71 27 | Budget–Moderate*

LEISURE, SPORT & BEACHES

BEACHES

The Bai Truong (Long Beach) on the west coast south of Duong Dong is a beautiful, approx. 20-km (12-mi) long, golden yellow, palm-fringed sandy strip, which

An endless beach paradise – Bai Truong

extends as far as the fishing harbour at *An Thoi* at the southern tip of the island. Some 4km (2.5mi) of it have been developed with bungalow complexes and hotels. It is unusual in that it's almost the only place in Vietnam where you can see the sun set from the beach. The beautifully arcing but remote beach at *Bai Ong Lang* (north of Duong Dong) is broken up by a series of sandy bays with rocky headlands. In the far south near An Thoi lie the snow-white powder sand and palm trees of *Bai Sao*.

DIVING

The fishermen in An Thoi or pleasure boats belonging to the hotels (from Bai Truong) will take tourists to the offshore islands, such as *Hon Doi Moi* or Turtle Island in the north (the best snorkelling is from *Bai Vung Bau beach)* and to the tiny *An Thoi archipelago* in the south, noted for the fine coral reefs in crystal clear water. With visibility up to 50m (Oct–April), the diving waters here rank among the best in Vietnam. During the diving season, *Rainbow Divers* organise PADI courses *(in Duong Dong at the start of Tran Hung Dao/Beach Rd or in the evening in the Rainbow Restaurant south of the Tropicana Resort by Bai Truong | mobile 09 13 40 09 64 | www.divevietnam.com).*

WALKING

You can walk to a number of small waterfalls and springs in the south east of Duong Dong, e.g. to *Suoi Tranh* spring, and also to caves and pepper plantations. The best time for excursions to the islands is during the dry season in winter.

WHERE TO STAY

INSIDER TIPP BEACH CLUB

Basic bungalow complex by the southern Bai Truong beach (6 rooms and 4 bungalows, all with sea view). Quiet beach restaurant, good information exchange point. *Tel. 077 3 98 09 98 | mobile 09 18 48 49 51 | www.beachclubvietnam.com | Budget*

MAI HOUSE

A quiet, tropical oasis with garden and palm-leaf-roofed bungalows and unusual furnishings in wood, terracotta, bamboo and rattan. No air-conditioning, no TV. *25 rooms | Bai Truong | tel. 077 3 84 70 03 | mobile 09 18 12 37 96 | Moderate*

MANGO BAY ☺

Eco-bungalows and wooden cabins beneath palm trees, some with open-air bath, ☼ verandas with sea view. Nice, airy seafood restaurant, rather rocky beach. *31 rooms | Bai Ong Lang | mobile 09 03 38 22 07 | www.mangobay phuquoc.com |Moderate–Expensive*

SAIGON PHU QUOC RESORT

This resort near the port has balcony rooms, suites, garden and beach bungalows, some with internet access and jacuzzi showers. Pool, children's playground, tennis court, karaoke disco, restaurants, bars. *43 rooms | Bai Truong | tel. 077 3 84 69 99 | www.vietnamphuquoc. com | Expensive*

LA VERANDA GRAND MERCURE RESORT & SPA

Boutique hotel with six luxurious villas. Large pool, French cuisine in a colonial-style restaurant. *43 rooms | Bai Truong | tel. 077 3 98 29 88 | www.accorhotels. com | Expensive*

INFORMATION

In the Saigon Phu Quoc Resort | 1 Tran Hung Dao | tel. 077 3 84 69 99 and 3 84 65 10 | www.phuquoc.info

WHERE TO GO

HA TIEN (136 A4) (*🗺 D12*)

Known as the Ha Long Bay of the south, Ha Tien is on the mainland. The town itself (pop. 40,000) is surrounded by hills and lies in a bay in the Gulf of Thailand. Since the border to nearby Cambodia was opened (approx. 10km/7mi away), more and more tourists have been passing through the town on their way along the coast to Thailand.

In the early 18th century, the Chinese Mac family pacified what was then a small settlement here, and built it up into a fiefdom. One survivor from that era is the ⚜ *Phao Dai* fortress with a view over the bay and the small *Dong Ho* or East Lake (not in fact a lake, but an inlet), which is squeezed between two granite cones known as the *Ngu Ho* and the *To Chau*. Elaborately decorated with dragon carvings, phoenixes, lion heads and guardian statues are the family tombs of the Mac dynasty, *Lang Mac Cuu*

(*Nui Lang | approx. 3km (2mi) northwest of the town centre, accessible via the Mac Tu Hoang*). In 1708, Prince Mac Cuu had allied himself with the Imperial family in Hue, which commissioned the tombs in 1802. Worshipped in the pretty pagoda, *Chua Tam Bao (Mac Thien Tich)* built between 1730–50, are the Goddess of Mercy, Quan Am, and the Jade Emperor. By the market and riverbank lies the highly-recommended *Xuan Thanh Restaurant (corner of Ben Tran Hau/Tham Tuong Sanh | tel. 077 3 85 21 97 | Budget)*. The *Hai Yen (85 rooms | 15 To Chau | tel. 077 3 85 15 80 | Budget)* is a bright, clean hotel (some rooms with refrigerator). If you are allocated one of the ⚜ corner rooms on the 3d or 4th floor, you will have the benefit of a fine view over the town. One small, green oasis with excellent all-round views is the ⚜ *Green Hill Guesthouse (9 rooms | 905 Hon Chong | Binh Anh | tel. 077 3 85 43 69 | Budget)*, which stands on a hill above Hon Chong Bay.

Roots and redemption – at the Mac dynasty tomb in Ha Tien

TRIPS & TOURS

The tours are marked in green in the road atlas,
the pull-out map and on the back cover

1 SEE THE MEKONG DELTA

Nine separate rivers flow through the delta into the South China Sea and that partly explains why the Vietnamese call the Mekong, the Song Cuu Long or the River of the Nine Dragons. Dragons because the mythical creatures symbolise life's driving force. This is where the magical appeal of tropical Vietnam is revealed. Rocking gently on the water between lush groves of palm trees beside the countless channels and tributaries are floating villages and markets, often reached only by simple, arched bridges, the so-called 'monkey bridges'. The boats lie close together, many of them full to the brim with rice and tea, aromatic spices or tropical fruits. A tour of the Mekong Delta is one of the highlights of a Vietnamese vacation. Allow at least three days to cover the 575-km (350-mi) long route.

The tour begins in Saigon → p. 81. Take the N 1A as far as the traffic-congested town of My Tho → p. 91. This city is an important trading and distribution centre for the millions of people who live in Saigon. Day after day they have to be supplied with rice, pineapples, bananas and oranges, all of which are grown in the Mekong Delta. Anything that is not dispatched to the nearby metropolis is sold by traders in the bustling market quarter. It is here, the gateway to the delta, where travellers with a limited amount of time can experience for them-

Photo: Mekong Delta

CONTENTS

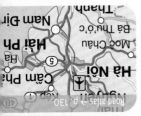

Saigon and the south → p. 76

Trips & Tours → p. 102

Sports & Activities → p. 108

Road atlas → p. 130

DID YOU KNOW?
Timeline → p. 12
Local specialities → p. 26
Books & Films → p. 52
Currency converter → p. 119
Budgeting → p. 120
Weather in Saigon → p. 122

MAPS IN THE GUIDEBOOK
(120 A1) Page numbers and coordinates refer to the road atlas
(O) Site/address located off the map. Coordinates are also given for places that are not marked on the road atlas
(U A1) Coordinates for the map of Ho Chi Minh City (Saigon) inside the back cover

INSIDE BACK COVER:
PULL-OUT MAP →

PULL-OUT MAP
(𝄜 A–B 2–3) Refers to the removable pull-out map
(𝄜 a–b 2–3) Refers to additional inset maps on the pull-out map

The best MARCO POLO Insider Tips

Our top 15 Insider Tips

INSIDER TIPP **Perspectives in black and white**
Long Thanh is one of Vietnam's best photographers. You can buy prints of his remarkable work in his gallery in Nha Trang → p. 29

INSIDER TIPP **Accommodation Vietnamese-style**
One little gem is the traditional-style *Viethouse Lodge*. Panoramic view of Ha Long included → p. 38

INSIDER TIPP **Limestone giants**
Ha Long Bay and *Lan Ha Bay* near Cat Ba have become Vietnam's most popular destination for rock climbers → p. 111

INSIDER TIPP **Smart eaterie**
This stylish mini-boutique hotel is a peaceful refuge in the at times chaotic Old Quarter of Hanoi. *Green Mango* serves exquisite Asian nouvelle cuisine – classic Vietnamese fare with some surprising 'fusions' → p. 47

INSIDER TIPP **Guesthouse in the hill town**
Spend the night in *Baguette & Chocolat* – not only will you eat well, you will also be supporting a worthwhile children's aid project → p. 52

INSIDER TIPP **Shopping spree**
Need a buddha for the terrace at home? *The Nguyen Frères shop* in Saigon is the perfect place to browse – it's tourist souvenir heaven. Everything from old furniture, objets d'art, jewellery and ceramics to pure kitsch → p. 87

INSIDER TIPP **South Seas magic**
Palm trees, soft sand and a crystal-clear sea – *Canh Duong Beach* near Da Nang → p. 62

INSIDER TIPP **Eat like an emperor**
Truc Lam Vien, a delightful garden restaurant in Da Nang, serves a wide range of tasty dishes → p. 62

INSIDER TIPP **Dinner and boat tour**
Combine Vietnamese fine dining with a cruise along the Thu Bon river *to the Red Bridge Restaurant* in Hoi An, ideally at sunset or under moonlight. You also get to see the fishermen at work → p. 66

INSIDER TIPP **Posh nosh Saigon-style**
The living room in an old villa belonging to the Vietnamese architect, Tran Binh, is the place to go in Saigon, if you want sumptuous, but traditional dining. Fine food served in the rarefied atmosphere of the Cuc Gach Quan – an intimate spot, ideal for special occasions. The proprietor sometimes sits by the pond in the garden smoking his pipe → p. 86

INSIDER TIPP **Jungle tour**
Visit Bach Ma National Park near Hue for breathtaking views over central Vietnam's mountains and at 'ground floor' level a wide range of fauna in the rain forest → p. 74

INSIDER TIPP **Enlightenment**
There's lots to see and do in Hoi An during the day. But every month on the 14th day of the lunar calendar, there's the Hoi An Legendary Night, when the narrow lanes are illuminated by the glow of Chinese lanterns, candles, tea lights and fairy lights → p. 65

INSIDER TIPP **Honeymoon dream & desert island**
Lonely, secluded, idyllic – a beach resort in luxurious rustic style. The villas of the *Evason Hideaway & Spa* are situated on a jungle peninsula near Nha Trang (photo left) → p. 95

INSIDER TIPP **Explore the underworld**
Amazing dripstone formations in *Phong Nha Cave* in central Vietnam → p. 108

INSIDER TIPP **A stage with no boards**
The ancient art of water puppetry – the best shows are in Hanoi (photo below) → p. 47

BEST OF ...

GREAT PLACES FOR FREE
Discover new places and save money

● *An early-morning work-out with the locals*
Join the early-bird athletes, who meet up every morning between 5am and 7am by *Lake Hoan Kiem* in Hanoi for sweat-inducing aerobics, badminton or a jog around the lake. You don't have to be a tai chi expert! In the evening hip-hop and break dancing take centre stage (photo) → p. 43

● *Queuing for Ho Chi Minh*
Tourists are invited to show reverence to the country's revered father figure, but they will have to join the queues outside Hanoi's *Ho Chi Minh Mausoleum*. Vietnamese people come from all over the country to shuffle respectfully past the glass sarcophagus → p. 43

● *Be a guest of the Jade Emperor*
Admission to the incense-shrouded world of the Taoists and their ruler Ngoc Hoang in his Saigon *pagoda* is completely free of charge. Pay your respects to the usual array of folk heroes, gods and demons → p. 82

● *Militarily precision – experience the 'old' Vietnam*
At 9pm on the dot, and with great military pomp, the Vietnamese flag is lowered on *Ba Dinh Square* in Hanoi. In today's turbo-capitalism it's a nostalgic trip down memory lane, providing a glimpse of the 'old' Vietnam with its Soviet-style parade ground discipline. → p. 43

● *Cross suspension bridges and wanders through the rice terraces*
Walk to *Cat Cat waterfall* with the beautiful scenery around the small mountain town of Sapa as the backdrop. It won't cost you anything – as long as you resist the sales pitches of the souvenir sellers along the route → p. 50

● *Insights into multi-colour world of the Cao Dai sect*
Admission to the main Cao Dai temple in Tay Ninh is not free. But you can visit the *Cao Dai temple* in Da Nang free of charge and even take part in a service – but you'll have to be as quiet as a mouse → p. 61

 Dots in guidebook refer to 'Best of ...' tips

ONLY IN VIETNAM
Unique experiences

● *In the footsteps of Confucius*
The *Van Mieu Temple of Literature* in Hanoi is the epitome of Confucian architecture. It was built 1,000 years ago in honour of the wise master. A very imposing structure and a must for any visitor to Vietnam → **p. 43**

● *Shake the wok!*
Hoi An without a *cookery course* is like a trip to Vietnam without buying a souvenir straw hat. There is no better place to learn how to prepare spring rolls or a hot pot. For sensory impressions at market and by the stove, try the Brother's Café → **p. 67**

● *Amphibious action on the Mekong*
Barges full of coconuts and rice, sampans with watchful eyes painted on the bow – the waterways of the Mekong Delta are like a marine motorway with *Cai Rang floating market* near Can Tho the service station. The hardest part is knowing where to start → **p. 78**

● *A cyclo adventure*
A tourist in a three-wheeler taxi might justifiably feel a little anxious, as the driver cycles straight into the mêlée at a congested crossroads – but as if by divine intervention a gap miraculously appears in the avalanche of sheet metal → **p. 82**

● *Dine like an emperor*
Be like the emperors of yesteryear and enjoy a nine-course royal dinner in the superb *Ancient Hue* restaurant → **p. 72**

● *David versus Goliath*
When you're on your Vietnam trip, don't miss the opportunity to crawl through Saigon's *Cu Chi tunnels*, the maze of underground galleries used by the Viet Cong. After this experience you will understand just a little better how a small, but determined David defeated the giant Goliath with its vast stocks of napalm bombs (photo) → **p. 90**

● *A look into the future*
The Vietnamese can see into your future. So what lies ahead? Ask a fortune teller from one of the hill tribes in Cao Bang or Sapa → **p. 36**

ONLY IN

BEST OF ...

● *All of Vietnam's ethnic groups at a glance*
The *Museum of Ethnology* in Hanoi provides a fascinating insight into the everyday lives of the many different peoples who make up Vietnam's population – you can even 'climb' inside one the traditional long houses (photo) → p. 42

● *Smells, crowds and noise*
Shop and eat until midnight in the large *Dong Xuan market hall* in the old quarter of Hanoi. Fresh fish and sweets, lacquer-ware, T-shirts and... karaoke! → p. 46

● *An Art Deco gem*
The summer palace of Bao Dai, Vietnam's last emperor, in Dalat is well worth a visit. A journey back in time on the creaking floorboards of 26 rooms → p. 58

● *Shiva, Ganesha & co.*
The *Cham Museum* in Da Nang houses an amazing collection documenting the culture of the Hindu Cham, who settled in central and south Vietnam 800 years ago. Look carefully at the sculptures and delicate reliefs and you can sense the strength of their religious faith → p. 61

● *Ho, Ho, Ho Chi Minh*
Perhaps rather sterile with too many glass displays, but still fascinating. It can be overrun by school groups and locals here to discover more about the life and work of the country's heroic revolutionary. In Saigon's *Dragon House* → p. 83

● *Shop until you drop*
If you think Vietnam is cheap, then treat yourself to a shopping spree in Saigon. The *Vincom Center* is a shopping mall with many famous designers and fashion brands from all over the world represented – no fakes, but expensive imports → p. 87

RAIN

RELAX AND CHILL OUT
Take it easy and spoil yourself

● *For foodies and chocoholics*
Need a break after morning sightseeing in Hanoi? Then check out the seemingly endless *chocolate buffet* in the Le Club café-restaurant in the legendary Sofitel Metropole → p. 48

● *Ice cream and violins*
Lick a hazelnut ice-cream or enjoy a *ca phe sua nong* to the sounds of piano and violin. Take it easy with something cool in the *Ca phe thu Bay* garden café in Saigon → p. 88

● *The spa treatment*
Jet lagged, stressed out from too much sightseeing or got blistered feet? Whatever you choose, whether it's gentle massaging hands or hot stones, warm chocolate or aromatic essences, after a pamper treatment at the *L'Apothiquaire Day Spa* you will feel fully renewed (photo) → p. 88

● *Chilling by the fire*
Surprised by the cold winter nights in Sapa? Warm yourself up by the fireplace in the cosy *Nature Bar & Grill* with a mulled wine and then choose from a range of hearty game dishes → p. 51

● *Cocktails & beach*
Feet buried in the sand sipping a mango margarita in the *Sandals Restaurant* beach bar – now that's how to see out a busy day → p. 97

● *A literary journey through Vietnam's colonial era*
Take a journey back in time, put Saigon's hurly-burly behind you and browse Graham Greene's classic 'The Quiet American' in style where it all happened – under the frangipani trees in the courtyard café of the venerable Hotel Continental → p. 89

● *Let yourself go*
Sit back on the sun deck and take a relaxing tour along the extensive network of rivers and channels that make up the Mekong Delta – preferably on a converted rice barge → p. 123

Monkey bridges, limestone rocks and mangrove forests – excursions to the Mekong Delta, Ha Long Bay and the national parks

selves the magic of the Mekong by taking a boat trip.

The landscape on the next stage to Vinh Long resembles one huge chessboard. Everywhere you look you will see rice paddies and dotted around in the flooded fields farmers in their distinctive straw hats hard at work. There's another fine market in **Vinh Long** (pop. 100,000). But in this case it's more typical of the delta. Seated in countless flat barges buyers and sellers are steered across the Tien Giang, one of the 'Nine Dragons'. The two

long wooden oars, operated crosswise from a standing position, look awkward to use, but rowers manoeuvre the boats with great skill.

Pure luxury is what travellers will get if they decide to stay in the *Victoria Hotel* in the provincial capital of **Can Tho → p. 77**. Why not stop off here, order a cocktail on the hotel terrace and watch events unfolding on the busy river? If you have time, hire your own boat and explore the labyrinthine residential quarter beside the often tiny side channels of the Hau

Giang. If there's no time for that, then a visit to Cai Rang floating market → p. 78 is a must, ideally as early in the day as possible.

Continue along the N 91, often peppered with potholes after heavy rain, into the Khmer region around Chau Doc → p. 80. The floating houses here are a distinctive feature of this little town. A nice way to round off a day's touring is to take an evening trip up Nui Sam Mountain → p. 80. Do also try to include in your schedule a stroll through the city with its ethnic mix of Moslems, Cham, Khmer and Vietnamese.

Another possible excursion could be to the Khmer village of Ba Chuc with its traditional temple, plus a rather grisly reminder of the barbarity of the Khmer Rouge in the Bone Pagoda. The skulls and bones of their victims are displayed as a memorial here. After the horror of Pol Pot's massacres, the unspoilt setting of the INSIDER TIPP Tra Su Reserve will be a welcome relief. Birders come here to watch thousands of white storks breeding. Now take the same route back to Saigon.

2 FROM HANOI TO THE WONDERS OF HA LONG BAY

Passing the many rice paddies, always following the Red River (Song Hong), this tour from Hanoi to the Gulf of Tonkin leads to one of Vietnam's finest natural spectacles: the petrified sugar loaves and limestone needles of Ha Long Bay. You will need at least two days for the 340km (210mi) journey on the busy roads around Hanoi. The best place to start is in Hanoi → p. 40 near the old post office by Lake Hoan Kiem. From here it's easy to reach the Chuong Dong bridge, which crosses the Red River as you make your way out of town. Now continue on the N 1 through the bustling district of Gia Lam and then take the N 5, which branches off to the right from the N 1 in four lanes. The residential area slowly thins and then the first dark green rice paddies come into view. So-named because of the reddish-brown heavily silt-laden waters, which flow for more than 1,800km (1,120mi), the Red River has created an extremely fertile region. After the heavy

Visitors welcome – Cham weaving village near Chau Doc

summer rains, it often overflows its banks and floods large parts of the area, hence the elaborate network of dykes and levees.

You are soon going to wonder why, stacked on wooden boards by the wayside, are bottles of soy sauce (tuong ban). Well, it is not far to Ban Yen Nhan. It is here in this village that the condiment, very popular among Vietnamese tourists, is made. It is now 59km (36mi) to the provincial capital of Hai Duong, home to another favourite delicacy, this time of the sweet variety. Known as banh dau xan, these are small, green or red coated sugary cakes made with mung bean flour. Another distinctive feature in the area are the brickworks, which you will see on both sides of the road. These factories now mass-produce the red roofing tiles, which in the past only the wealthy could afford.

Just beyond Hai Duong, the road branches off to the left to Sao Do, before you reach the small town of Dong Trieu. If you have a penchant for INSIDER TIPP fine pottery, you might find something of exquisite beauty here, because Dong Trieu is an important centre of Vietnam's ceramics industry.

Suddenly it appears on the horizon: the breathtaking sight of Ha Long Bay → p. 35. When you first see those 2,000 or so towering limestone rocks, the legend of the 'descending dragon' (ha long) may not seem quite so fanciful. The starting point for a boat ride lasting several hours is the tourist centre of Bai Chay. To cope with the stampede of tourists, Bai Chay, and the town just north of it, Hon Gai have merged to form Ha Long City. Within a few minutes of leaving the port, you will have forgotten about the chaotic scramble in the city. Instead, you will be captivated by the magical spectacle of this unique seascape of tall, rocky out-

crops. There is hardly a rock that hasn't been given a special name that in some way matches its shape. It's easy to identify Camel Island or Turtle Island. Others are less obvious.

Return to Hanoi by the same route.

3 A MANGROVE FOREST AND A NATIONAL PARK – A TOUR INTO VIETNAM'S GREEN HEARTLAND

This 700-km (425-mi) long route is one of the most varied tours you can make in Vietnam. It takes about a week (at least 5 days) to travel from the country's first Unesco Biosphere Reserve of Can Gio near the south Vietnamese metropolis of Saigon to one of the most species-diverse jungle national parks (Cat Tien), then into the perhaps more climatically agreeable central highlands near Dalat, before returning via a stunning mountain pass to the coast at the seaside resort of Nha Trang. On the way you will be able to observe birds, ride on an elephant, visit hill tribe settlements and marvel at the ruins left by the 13th-century Cham rulers. It is advisable to make this trip during the dry season, i.e. between November/December and March/April.

The tour of the lush green countryside starts 55km (35mi) southeast of the sprawling, 7 million strong city of Saigon. An 'island' formed by the alluvial sands of the Saigon River, Can Gio (approx. 800sq km/300sq mi) is best known for its mangrove forest. It was also the first of Unesco's biosphere reserves in Vietnam. During the Vietnam War, the trees were destroyed by the Americans using the defoliant known as Agent Orange, a highly toxic dioxin. Happily, over recent decades, this saline wetland has been re-forested and it has now more or less fully

Noted for its top-class coffee beans – the coffee harvest in Buon Ma Thuot

recovered. The mangrove forest with its trees on stilt roots today offers a safe habitat for lots of fish species, birds and reptiles, such as monitor lizards. A colony of several hundred macaques also lives here. You can stay in basic guesthouses or a mid-range hotel by the beach, but at the weekend it can resemble carnival time *(visit www.cangioresort.com.vn for what is described as 'eco tourism' in Can Gio resort in the village of Long Hoa – but what exactly is meant by 'eco' here is not at all clear... tel. 08 38 74 33 35)*. On the south side lies an approx. 10-km (6-mi) long, but perhaps rather coarse and windy beach, but it is the closest one to Saigon. A handful of food stalls here serve fresh fish and seafood.

Now continue your journey towards Saigon in a northeasterly direction on the N 1. After about 30km (20mi) through what is the seemingly endless industrial suburb of Bien Hoa, you might like to take a short break. The town is a handicrafts centre and there are shops that sell the artisans' products. Beyond Bien Hoa near the km 69 marker in Dau Giay, turn right off the N 1 on to the N 20, which leads inland up into the mountains, initially passing rubber plantations and fields of fruit trees. On the Tri An reservoir (also called Lake La Nga) live many fishermen in houseboats and also in floating villages. About 70km (43mi) beyond Tan Phu, turn left along a track toward Cat Tien National Park → p. 90. There is accommodation in guesthouses or in the smart, but rustic-style Forest Floor Lodge *(www.vietnamforesthotel.com)*.

Now take a rough track from the National Park (in the rainy season only possible by four-wheel drive) towards the N 20 and Ma Da Gui. The road slowly winds its way up to an altitude of 1,500m (5,000ft), crossing then into the province of Lam Dong, where dense jungle finally envelops the pass. Visible from the road are a number of pretty temple shrines and waterfalls. You reach the upland plateau near the small town of Bao Loc → p. 60, where popular tourist attractions include tea factories and silkworm farms. There are also some spectacular waterfalls here, well worth a detour: the

Dambri waterfall (near Bao Loc) and the **Pongour waterfall** (near Duc Trong, about 45km (28mi) south of Dalat). After the creation of the huge Nhim reservoir north of Dalat, the once magnificent falls and pretty lakes in and around Dalat lost a lot of their water – and so the best time to visit the cascades here is at the end of the rainy season (Nov/Dec).

Hoardings plastered with posters, giant greenhouses and plastic sheeting by the N 20 herald the proximity of the mountain town of **Dalat → p. 58**, the favourite destination for Vietnamese honeymooners.

If you have enough time, then you could take a multi-day detour south of Dalat on the N 27 to the west, to the less tourist-orientated capital of Dak Lak province, **Buon Ma Thuot → p. 56**, a town renowned for its coffee, said to be the best in Vietnam. Leave Buon Ma Thuot and head toward the coast and Nha Trang, the end of the tour.

If you haven't got time to include Buon Ma Thuot in your itinerary, go east out of Dalat to Phan Rang along the winding N 20 and then turn on to the N 27 towards the coast. You will pass the **Da Nhim reservoir** and a huge hydro-electric power station. The scenically rewarding **Ngoan Muc pass** – if the weather is fine you can even see the coast some 60km (37mi) away – snakes its way from an altitude of around 1,000m (3250ft) down to the coastal plain, where once again palm trees and cacti dominate the landscape. Perched on a hill a few kilometres from the coastal town of **Phan Rang**, you can see the well preserved Cham temples dating from the 13th and 14th centuries, namely **Po Klong Garai → p. 59** and **Po Rome**, the latter approx. 15km (10mi) south of Phan Rang. Now take the N 1 north to the resort of **Nha Trang → p. 92**. On the way you will pass two other Cham towers (Hoa Lai); further north is the **port of Cam Ranh**, from 1964 to 1973 an important US naval base. On this last stretch you could take a meal break at one of the seafront restaurants on stilts.

Nha Trang – the end of the tour

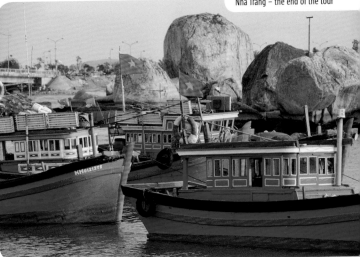

SPORTS & ACTIVITIES

The range of activity holidays in Vietnam is gradually widening. But don't expect perfection – facilities for many of the leisure pursuits, tours or 'soft adventures', such as caving, are still fairly rudimentary.

Safety standards at some Vietnamese companies are still rudimentary. The cheaper the tour (kayaking or rock climbing, for example), the more inexperienced the guides are likely to be.

CAVING

Keen cavers love exploring the 14 vast chambers in the INSIDER TIPP Phong Nha Cave, the largest and finest cave in Vietnam (under Unesco protection since 2003). It is located close to Son Trach, 55km (34mi) northwest of Dong Hoi in central Vietnam. Caving tours and motorcycle or jeep excursions to the old Ho Chi Minh Trail are organised by Phong Nha Farmstay together with tour operator Oxalis Adventures. When they set up Farmstay, Australian Ben and his Vietnamese wife Bich aimed to create a INSIDER TIPP small and friendly centre, where guests can socialise with the family. Pool, no air conditioning, book early. *Cu Nam | Dong Hoi | tel. 052 3 67 51 35 | mobile 094 4 75 98 64 | phong-nha-cave.com | Budget–Moderate | tour approx. 1,000,000 dong (further information: www.oxalis.com. vn/GL/en/home, includes YouTube caving film).* You can visit the cave by boat (admission 100,000 dong, boat for up

Active holiday enthusiasts will be breaking new ground in Vietnam, but they can still look forward to adventure aplenty

to 10 people about 200,000 dong). Another tried-and-tested tour operator is *Footprint Vietnam Travel (6 Le Thanh Ton | Hanoi | tel. 04 39 33 28 44 | www. footprintsvietnam.com).*

COOKERY COURSES

Clearly plenty of visitors to Hoi An stir the pot – or more correctly the wok – at least once during a stay –, so that they can prepare and serve pho lau or cao lau at home.

Many restaurants (including in Hanoi and Saigon) offer cookery courses of varying lengths, some with market visit *(half day from about 400,000 dong per person, subject to number of participants).* You could try any of the following: *Vy's Cooking School* in the Morning Glory Restaurant *(tel. 0510 2 24 15 56 | www.restaurant-hoian.com),* the Brothers Café, Red Bridge Restaurant *(all day | www.visithoian.com),* Tam Tam Café and Lighthouse *(www.lighthousecafehoian. com).*

CYCLING

Ideally, cyclists should bring their own bike and also a good selection of spare parts. Good bikes (rental costs approx. 30,000 to 60,000 dong per day) are rare in Vietnam, as are bike shops with a good supply of spare parts. The Hanoi to Saigon route (or vice versa) is popular, as scenically it is very varied; apart from the Cloud Pass , the route does not make any strenuous demands on fitness. The main problem, however, is the chaotic, sometimes dangerous, traffic on the N 1. Information: *Footloose Adventure Travel | 3 Springs Pavement, Ilkley, West Yorkshire | 00 44 1943 60 40 30 | www.footlooseadventure.co.uk | www. cyclingvietnam.net | www.biking-asia.com*

DIVING

Nha Trang and Phu Quoc are the best sites in Vietnam for diving. Nha Trang boasts a number of diving schools. Visibility here is on average 15m (50ft), during the dry season up to 30m (100ft), in Phu Quoc up to 50m (160ft). Currently there are about 25 dive sites and an artificial wreck is planned. In addition to relatively well-preserved hard and soft cor-als, there are also tropical fish as well as sand sharks and oceanic white-tip sharks. Two dives (one tank each) from approx. 1,100,000 dong. Further information: *Rainbow Divers | www.divevietnam.com*

GOLF

Golf is the latest craze in the 'new Vietnam'. There are several golf courses suitable for both professional and amateur players, such as the ones near Hanoi and Saigon, in Phan Thiet and in Dalat. *www. oceandunesgolf.vn*

KAYAK TOURS

By far the best is the INSIDER TIPP sea kayak tour through Ha Long Bay. You can choose from tours of between 1 and 6 days in length, all with an English-speaking escort. Some 6–8km (4–5mi) covered per day, depending on the fitness level of the group and number of caves to be visited. On multi-day tours, overnight stops in tents; luxury offers include accommodation on a boat. Two-day tours including meals cost from around 5,000,000 dong per person; book through a reputable tour opera-

Adventures on water – canoeing

tor, e.g. *SeaCanoe and Inserimex Travel* (www.johngray-seacanoe.com).

ROCK CLIMBING

INSIDER TIPP Ha Long Bay and Lan Ha Bay near Cat Ba are the perfect destinations for dedicated rock climbers. The views are terrific, the challenges great. But if you want to climb independently, you must bring your own equipment. You also need the experience of pilots and guides, who know the tides, as access to many of the caves and lagoons inside the giant limestone rocks is only possible when the water is at a certain level. Information and tours (with trained climbers and equipment): *Slo Pony Adventures | 1/4 Street No. 4 (c/o Noble House Guest House) | Cat Ba | tel. 031 3 68 84 50 | mobile 09 03 47 34 01 | www.slopony.com | day tours approx. 1,250,000 dong*

SAILING

There is no organised sailing in Vietnam yet. But if you want to get out on the water, then **INSIDER TIPP** *Whale Island Resort (tel. 058 3 84 05 01),* off Nha Trang, can offer a number of maritime

activities. You can learn how to handle a catamaran; windsurfing and canoes also available. Information and booking via *Découvrir (www.iledelabaleine.com).*

TAI CHI

If you are interested in the Chinese martial art of tai chi or thai cuc quyen in Vietnamese, you will have to get up early. For the equivalent of a few pence, you can join courses in Saigon: Tue–Sat 5.30am–7am and 7am–8.30pm in *Le Van Tam Park (Hai Ba Trung/corner Dien Bien Phu).*

WINDSURFING

One excellent windsurfing beach is Mui Ne near Phan Thiet. Competitions such as the *Starboard Vietnam Fun Cup are staged here.* For more information contact *Jibe Club Mui Ne | www.windsurf-vietnam.com.* All the action starts in the *Full Moon Beach Resort (km 13.5 marker | Ham Tien | Mui Ne | tel. 062 3 84 70 08).* A windsurfing package for one week, including half-board and board rental, costs around 8,000,000 dong. Leisure pursuits on offer at the *Mia Resort (24 Nguyen Dinh Chieu | Mui Ne | tel. 062 3 84 74 40 | www.miamuine.com)* include surfing and kite surfing.

WALKING

The best areas for walking are the Bach Ma National Park, the hilly area around Sapa, the Ba Be National Park as well as the uplands near Dalat , e.g. Mount Lang Bian. You will need to bring your own equipment, e.g. boots, walking sticks, rucksack, water bottles, energy bars. (You can buy high-quality trekking equipment in Saigon, Hanoi and Sapa.) Recommended: *Phat Tire Ventures (73 Truong Cong Dinh | Dalat | tel. 063 3 82 94 22 | mobile 09 18 43 87 81 | www.phattireventures.com).*

TRAVEL WITH KIDS

All tay – Westerners – are made very welcome in Vietnam, but those travelling with their own children even more so. Children usually find there is plenty to keep them entertained. In Hanoi and in Saigon, for example, the superb water puppet theatre performances always get a good reception.

Children up to two years of age (or less than 0.80m) can usually fly free of charge in Vietnam and, in many situations, children up to 10 years of age are granted a reduction of up to 50 percent, e.g. coach tours, excursions or amusement parks. Saigon and Hanoi and also Phan Thiet, Mui Ne and Nha Trang are well catered for holidaymakers and so make ideal bases for family vacations. The latter resort is very popular, because it has such beautiful, soft sandy beaches.

ELEPHANT RIDES
Older children will love the two-hour elephant ride by Lake Lak (137 E2) *(₥ G11)* (from Buon Jun village) or from the elephant village of Ban Don (137 E1) *(₥ G10)*. Two to three people can sit on one animal, which can wade comfortably through the shallow lake. Information and booking: *Dak Lak Tourist in Buon Ma Thuot | 53 Ly Thuong Kiet | tel. 0500 3 85 22 46 | www.daklak tourist.com.vn*

HANOI SUPER KARTING CENTRE (0) *(₥ 0)*
Always a winner with older children (and young-at-heart parents). Whiz around in a go-kart for approx. 80,000 dong. *Thanh Nhan Youth Park*

LAKE DA THIEN (137 E2) *(₥ G11)*
Surrounded by a hills some 5km (3mi) north of Dalat is the 'Valley of Love'. It might initially sound romantic, but it is in fact an amusement park with countless souvenir shops. Attractions include pony rides, canoes and pedalos. *Daily 8am–6pm | admission 6,000 dong*

ON THE ROAD
Do remember to come equipped with plenty of sunscreen and suitable clothing, including some form of sun hat. The sun block must be of a factor high enough to provide protection from the fierce, tropical sun. Parents of very young children should pack pacifiers, bottles, glasses and a couple of terry cloth reusable nappies. A baby carrier is certainly useful for overland travel, but on the other hand

The family unit is valued highly in Vietnam – so younger travellers are always welcome

you should keep luggage volumes to a minimum, particularly if travelling on cramped tourist buses.

Everyone, especially children, should drink lots of fluids, but on no account tap water. For reasons of hygiene, only eat ice-cream in a luxury hotel, but it's safer not to buy it all. It's nearly always possible to rustle up the usual children's staples, such as French fries, ketchup and coke.

TOYS

If your child loses his or her beloved teddy bear, you might be lucky and find an identical one to replace it. But how about one in a Superman outfit or one dressed as a baby panda? Many unusual toys are available in the following shops in Saigon: *Wooden Toys (Diamond Plaza Shopping Center, 37 Le Duan | (U D3) (f d3), 142 A Ly Chinh Thang | (U B2) (f b2))* or in *Kids like us in Hanoi (39 Nguyen Thai Hoc | opposite Brothers Café | (138 B4).*

WATER PARKS

Hanoi Water Park covers an area of nearly 10 acres *(daily 7.30am–7pm | 614 Lac Long Can, West Lake | (0) (∅ 0) | admission approx. 80,000 dong)* and has many swimming pools and giant slides. The *Dam Sen Water Park (Mon–Fri 9am–6pm, Sat, Sun 7am–7pm | 3 Hoa Binh | (0) (∅ 0) | www.damsenwaterpark.com. vn | admission approx. 80,000 dong)* in Saigon is an amusement park with rides to suit all age groups, e.g. rowing boats, giant water slide, *Space Spiral* and a children's railway, likewise in Nha Trang. There is usually a quieter zone for foreigners, but don't expect western standards.

ZOOS

You will find zoos and animal parks in many Vietnamese cities and they make popular days out for families with children. However, it has to be said that the animals are often kept in miserable conditions.

FESTIVALS & EVENTS

1 Jan: *Christian New Year (Tet Duong Lich),* **3 Feb:** *Founding of the Vietnamese Communist Party (1930);* **30 April***: Liberation Day (fall of Saigon to the North Vietnamese forces in 1975),* **1 May***: May Day;* **19 May***: Ho Chi Minh's birthday (1890),* **2 Sept***: National Day (Declaration of Independence 1945)*

NATIONAL FESTIVALS BASED ON THE LUNAR CALENDAR

Most traditional festivals follow the Chinese lunar calendar. As the lunar month is only 29 or 30 days and the lunar year has 354 or 355 days, every three years between the third and fourth lunar month an extra month is added (a table converting the lunar year to the solar calendar and vice versa can be found at *www.vietnamtourism.com,* Tourism/Festivals).

TET NGUYEN DAN

The Chinese and Vietnamese New Year is the most important family event. Celebrations can go on for a week. Flights get booked up very quickly. (1st day of the 1st month; 10 February 2013, 31 Jan 2014)

THANH MINH

The Vietnamese people decorate the graves of their relatives with flowers, candles and paper money. (5th day of the 3rd month; 14 April 2013, 4 April 2014)

PHAT DAN

Buddha's birthday is celebrated with processions to the Buddhist pagodas. (8th day of the 4th month; 17 May 2013, 6 May 2014)

TET DOAN NGO

The midsummer festival begins with the symbolic burning of paper sculptures – to drive away the bad spirits from people afflicted with a disease. The risk of epidemics is said to be at its greatest at the height of summer. (5th day of the 5th month; 12 June 2013, 2 June 2014)

TRUNG NGUYEN

In the hope that the wandering souls of the long-forgotten dead have no negative impact on an individual's fate, for this holiday offerings in the form of gifts and food are made to altars at home and in temples. (15th day of the 7th month; 31 Aug 2012, 21 Aug 2013, 10 Aug 2014)

The ancestors, the gods and the spirits have to be honoured – many of Vietnam's colourful celebrations follow the lunar calendar

TRUNG THU ⭐

The mid-autumn festival, also known as the children's moon festival, is celebrated with lantern processions at night under a full moon. Children are given special, moon-shaped sticky rice cakes. This is also the time to celebrate engagements and weddings. (15th day of the 8th month; 30 Sept 2012, 19 Sept 2013, 8 Sept 2014)

LOCAL FESTIVALS BASED ON THE LUNAR CALENDAR

SPRING AND AUTUMN

If you travel throughout the country in spring or autumn, everywhere, but mainly in the villages, you will see colourful flags – they herald the ▶ ⭐ *Le Hoi festivals*. Le Hoi day is considered the most important event in every village's annual cycle. It is held to honour the village's guardian spirit. After a procession the villagers present a sacrificial offering to the spirit. After that, a lavish banquet is held or plays and concerts performed. One spectacular celebration is ▶ *Le Hoi Choi Trau,* the village festival in Do Son (25km/16mi southeast of Hai Phong). After a prelude of music and dancing, two water buffaloes are pitted against each other until one gives up. The owner of the winning buffalo receives a cash prize and then the animal is sacrificed to the harvest god. (8/9th day of the 8th month; 23/24th Sept 2012, 12/13 Sept 2013, 1/2nd Sept 2014)

APRIL/MAY

To mark the ▶ *Huong Tich festival* grand pilgrimages to the temples of Huong Tich Son take place. (15th day of the 3rd month; 24 April, 2013, 14 April 2014)

LINKS, BLOGS, APPS & MORE

LINKS

▶ www.livinginvietnam.com If you want to know what's going on, ask someone who lives there. News, accommodation, jobs, communities and articles by expats – a good source of information on the practicalities of life in Vietnam

▶ www.vietnamadventures.com Another excellent site full of practical information. Features monthly adventures and good travel deals

▶ www.vietnamonline.com Lots of useful travel information, including Destinations and Travel Tools, Blogs and Videos

▶ www.thingsasian.com/vietnam One of the best and most colourful sites, covering all aspects of life and travelling in Vietnam. From Adoption to Women & Travel, with travelogues, photos, etc

▶ www.360cities.net The 360° panoramic photos give an all-round view of top sights. Check out the rotating views of the Mekong Delta, Phong Nha Cave, Ha Long Bay, Hoi An by night, even Saigon General Post Office

▶ www.panoramio.com A photo-sharing website linked to Google Maps. Enter the place you want to visit in the search field and then take a peep at other people's holiday snaps

▶ www.responsible-travel.org Not Vietnam-specific, but an excellent primer with plenty of commonsense advice. Check out the pages on Bargaining or Begging

BLOGS & FORUMS

▶ www.alloexpat.com/vietnam_expat_forum This active site covers most aspects of the expatriate's lifestyle

▶ vietnamesegod.blogspot.com Van Cong Tu is a food blogger and local hospitality industry insider from Nha Trang, currently living in Hanoi. His culinary adventures in Vietnam are recorded in this internet diary. Entries go back to 2005

Regardless of whether you are still preparing your trip or already in Vietnam: these addresses will provide you with more information, videos and networks to make your holiday even more enjoyable

VIDEOS, STREAMS & PODCASTS

▶ http://vimeo.com Sign up to Vimeo and search for 'traffic in Hanoi' or 'cooking class in Hoi An'. These two and others provide a revealing insight into the real Vietnam

▶ www.huongthanh.com Contemporary music by popular singer Huong Thanh. Melancholic sounds in traditional style, perfect for a boat trip through a misty Ha Long Bay

▶ http://www.battlesofwar.com Memories of the Vietnam War are fading and the combatants and the civilians who survived probably would in any case prefer to forget about it. However, this footage is a grim reminder of its horrors

▶ http://podcast.eastmanhouse.org/ghosts-in-the-landscape-vietnam-revisited From a George Eastman House exhibition. An ex-marine returns to Vietnam to revisit some of his former military routes

▶ http://survivalphrases.com/vietnamese Get the first ten rudimentary phrases for free. Then sign up for the next stage. Available as podcasts

APPS

▶ If you want to improve your Vietnamese via an app on your smart phone, Worldnomads, Rosetta Stone, L-Lingo, Lingvosoft are the brand names you'll come across. Take your pick!

▶ http://itunes.apple.com/us/app/vietnamese-recipes Find delicious Vietnamese recipes with this recipe app. Ingredients listed and then the next steps are explained

NETWORKS

▶ www.couchsurfing.org Describes itself as the largest traveller community. You don't have to sign up to find profiles of travellers or locals. Click 'Browse People' and then enter 'Vietnam' in the search field

▶ www.twitter.com Twitter is well established in Vietnam too

▶ www.lonelyplanet.com/thorntree Travel forum with lots of practical tips. Helps newcomers and others plan their trips to Vietnam

TRAVEL TIPS

ARRIVAL

✈ Vietnam Airlines fly non-stop every day from London to Saigon and Hanoi (approx. £600). A number of airlines, including Vietnam Airlines, Qatar Airways and American Airlines, fly from New York, Los Angeles and other cities (from 800US$). When booking onward flights within Vietnam or to neighbouring countries, the Vietnamese national carrier often grants a discount of 50 percent. *www.vietnamairlines.com*

BANKS, MONEY & CURRENCY

Opening times for Vietnamese banks are normally as follows: Mon–Fri 7.30am–11.30am and 1.30pm–3.30pm or 4pm. However, these times can often vary.

Even if prices are given in US dollars, always pay in the local currency, the Vietnam dong (VND). There are ATM machines in all towns and you can use your Visa and MasterCard cards to draw Vietnamese dong from them, but you should expect to pay a small fee. You can change dollars and travellers' cheques without any problem (make sure you have your passport with you). Large hotels, tourist restaurants, travel agencies and airline offices accept credit cards (1 to 3 percent handling fee). For safety's sake, it's a good idea to keep a few US dollars and some travellers' cheques on you, particularly if you're planning to move on to Cambodia or are likely to arrive at Hanoi airport late at night.

Always check the digits when handling Vietnamese dong polymer notes. They range in value from 500 to 1,000,000 VND. For everyday transactions use the 10,000 (£0.30/0.40US$), 50,000, 100,000 notes and in more expensive restaurants the 500,000 note (£15/25US$).

The official bank exchange rate is often less favourable (by approx. 2500 VND) at the airport, in hotels and in large towns. It is safe to you use the licensed, privately-run change bureaux (usually open from 7am–10pm, e.g. in Dong Khoi street or in Saigon's General Post Office) or in larger jewellery shops.

As the theft of smaller sums of money from rooms, luggage, even room safes, is not uncommon, if possible leave your money in the safe at reception and ask for a receipt.

RESPONSIBLE TRAVEL

It doesn't take a lot to be environmentally friendly whilst travelling. Don't just think about your carbon footprint whilst flying to and from your holiday destination but also about how you can protect nature and culture abroad. As a tourist it is especially important to respect nature, look out for local products, cycle instead of driving, save water and much more. If you would like to find out more about eco-tourism please visit: *www.ecotourism.org*

CONSULATES & EMBASSIES

UK EMBASSY HANOI
Central Building, 4th floor | 31 Hai Ba Trung | Hanoi | tel. 04 39 36 05 00 | http://ukinvietnam.fco.gov.uk/en/

From arrival to weather

Holiday from start to finish: the most important addresses and information for your Vietnam trip

UK CONSULATE SAIGON

25 Le Duan Street | District 1 | Saigon | tel. 08 38 25 13 80

US EMBASSY HANOI

2nd floor | Rose Garden Tower 170 | Ngoc Khanh Street | Hanoi | http://vietnam. usembassy.gov

US CONSULATE SAIGON

4 Le Duan Blvd. Dist. 1 | Saigon | tel. 35 0 20 42 00 | http://hochiminh.usconsu late.gov

CUSTOMS

1.5l of high-percentage alcohol or 2l wine and 400 cigarettes or 100 cigars or 500g tobacco may be imported into Vietnam duty-free. If you wish to export antiques, you will need to obtain an export certificate. The following quantities may be imported into EU (per person aged 18 or above): 200 cigarettes, 50 cigars or 250g tobacco, 1l alcohol above and 2l alcohol up to 22 vol.%, 500g coffee, other goods such as tea, perfume and gifts up to a value of £390/574US$.

ELECTRICITY

Mains voltage is usually 220V. Remember to pack a universal adapter.

HEALTH

No vaccinations are required, unless you have arrived from a yellow-fever zone. However, protection against polio, tetanus, diphtheria, hepatitis A/B and typhus is recommended. A stand-by medication, e.g. Lariam or Malarone, is advisable in malaria regions. To avoid diarrhoea, do not drink tap water or even use it to clean your teeth. Do not eat unpeeled fruit or salad, unless you are dining in an international hotel. The same advice applies to ice-cream. Because of the risk of cholera in north Vietnam (mainly Hanoi and Ninh Binh), it is probably better to avoid it altogether. Vaccination against cholera is no longer a requirement for entry into any country, but an oral vaccine against cholera is available. If you consider yourself to be at risk, contact your doctor. Den-

CURRENCY CONVERTER

£	VND	VND	£
1	33,600	10000	0.30
2	67,000	20000	0.60
3	100,000	30000	0.90
4	135,000	40000	1.20
5	168,000	50000	1.50
6	200,000	60000	1.80
7	235,000	70000	2.10
8	269,000	80000	2.40
9	302,000	90000	2.70

$	VND	VND	$
1	21,000	10000	0.48
2	42,000	20000	0.96
3	63,000	30000	1.44
4	84,000	40000	1.92
5	105,000	50000	2.40
6	125,000	60000	2.88
7	146,000	70000	3.36
8	167,000	80000	3.84
9	187,000	90000	4.32

For current exchange rates see www.xe.com

gue fever has been reported in the south of Vietnam, mainly in the Mekong Delta region, but also in other parts of the country. The virus is transmitted by a mosquito, which is active during the daytime. The best form of prevention is to wear bright, long-sleeved clothing and use a mosquito repellent. There is no vaccine. For up-to-date information, contact your doctor's

BUDGETING

Coffee	£0.35 / 0.50 $
	for one cup in a Vietnamese café
Noodle soup	£1 / 1.50 $
	in a Vietnamese restaurant
Taxi ride	£0.25 / 0.40 $
	per kilometre
Beer	From approx. £0.85 / 1.30 $
	for a draught beer in a Vietnamese bar
Dress	£12–£20 / 20–35 $
	for an ao dai dress
Massage	£2 / 3 $
	on the beach

surgery or consult the website of a hospital specialising in tropical medicine. A health insurance policy is essential. Make sure cover includes medical evacuation costs.

INFORMATION

ICS TRAVEL GROUP
870 Market Street, Suite 923 | San Francisco, CA 94102 | USA | Tel. 0415 434 4015 | www.indochina-services.com

VIETNAM TOURISM
30 A Ly Thuong Kiet | Hanoi | tel. 04 38 25 99 42 | www.vietnamtourism.com | www.vietnamtourism-info.com | www.vietnamtourism.gov.vn

SAIGON TOURIST
– 55 B Phan Chu Trinh | Hanoi | tel. 04 38 25 09 23
23 Le Loi | Saigon District 1 | tel. 08 38 29 22 91 | www.saigontourist.net | www.saigon-tourist.com

FOCUS ASIA
235/3 VO Thi Sau | Saigon | tel. 08 39 32 07 32 | www.focus-asia.biz
If you want to know whether there is a tourist office where you are staying, ask at your hotel.

NEWSPAPERS

There are two English-language newspapers: Saigon Times Weekly and Vietnam News *(www.vietnamnews.com.vn)*. Most large hotels, international bookshops and street vendors in town centres sell the main foreign press titles. Tourists often find Time Out Vietnam and The Guide useful.

OPENING TIMES & ADMISSION CHARGES

Do not expect opening times to be punctually adhered to. Many places of interest are open at all times, some are even open in the evening. Unless otherwise stated, admission is free.

PHONE & MOBILE PHONE

The country code for the UK is 0044, USA 001 and Vietnam 0084. Then dial the local area code without the zero, followed by the number you are calling. Calling abroad from your hotel can cost less than £0.80 (1.20US$) per minute using VoIP codes, e.g. 171, so for the UK, it's

1710044. Normal hotel self-dial connections, i.e. landline Vietnam to landline UK, cost approx. £1.20 (1.90US$) per minute. However, the 171 prefix does not work in all hotels. It is often cheaper to use an IDD phone obtainable from post offices and some telephone kiosks (up to approx. £0.30/0.50US$ per minute). Cheapest of all are the internet cafés (e.g. with Skype or Yahoo! Voice it's free, but often with poor connections. Turning off the webcam can help to improve sound quality). The mobile phone providers are *Vinaphone (www.vinaphone.com.vn)* and *Mobiphone (www.mobifone.com.vn)*. Using a foreign SIM card in Vietnam can be expensive. If you are using a British or American provider, extra hidden charges are added by the Vietnamese companies to incoming calls, in some cases up to £0.80 (1.20US$) per minute. For information on the roaming agreement: *www.gsmworld.com*. One way to save money on calls home is to buy a prepaid 1718 card, so when you use the low-cost code 1718 (+0044), a call to the UK can cost as little as 2,000 VND (£0.08/0.13US$ per minute).

A much cheaper option is get family members or friends to call you back. From the UK and USA to Vietnam (landline and mobile): either via Skype or with scratch cards obtainable in Asian food shops. With the latter, you can speak for approx. 240 minutes for £5/8US$, e.g. *www.nobelphonecard.com* or *www.nobelphonecard.uk*. With a Vietnamese SIM card *(£2.50–£12.50/4–20US$ for the card with approx. £5/8US$ credit)*, you can phone to the Europe and North America for approx. £0.15 (0.25US$) per minute and send text messages *(approx. £0.08/0.13US$)*, however you will need an unlock code and you will be allocated a new telephone number. As there are wide variety of expensive telephone numbers in Vietnam (e.g. the expensive, but easy to remember 4 00 40 04 00), INSIDER TIPP when you buy, make sure you ask for a 'cheap' number.

POST

Airmail deliveries to Europe and the USA can take up to three weeks (a stamp for a postcard is approx. £0.35/0.50US$). Only post letters or cards in post offices in the larger towns or in quality hotels. If you want to send a parcel, it can be expensive and unreliable. Better to use a courier service, such as DHL (counter in Saigon General Post Office).

TAXI & RICKSHAW

In Hanoi and in Saigon, many taxis have taximeters (approx. £0.25/0.40US$ per km) with the taximeter set to 11,000 VND when you start your journey. Unfortunately, some taxi drivers in Hanoi and Saigon do use various tricks to swindle their passengers. Often 'false' taxis are fitted with doctored taximeters, so that the fare for a journey within the city can end up amounting to several million VND. If the figure on the taximeter appears to be rising rapidly and the driver keeps beeping his horn, ask him to stop, pay the stated sum and get out quickly. If you want a taxi from your hotel, order an official taxi or only use official, reputable companies. In Saigon *Vinasun* and *Vinataxi* are reliable as are *May Linh* throughout Vietnam (hotline: 08 38 27 79 79). Cyclos, i.e. cycle-hauled rickshaws, are cheap and environmentally-friendly, but it is normal to negotiate a price in advance. Moped taxis are also popular (always wear a helmet). In many cities, such as Can Tho, there are such things as motorised cyclo taxis, i.e. a moped in front of a two-seater carriage). As it is difficult for tourists to figure out how the rather sparse public bus service operates (only in Saigon and Hanoi) and Saigon's underground is not due to be completed until 2015/16, the taxi in all its different manifestations will for some time yet continue to be the main way of getting around.

TIME

Vietnam time is seven hours ahead of Greenwich Mean Time, during the summer only six hours ahead; it is 15 hours ahead of Standard Pacific Time and 12 hours ahead of Eastern Standard Time.

TIPPING

Feel free to tip good service, but in the better-class restaurants and hotels, it is often retained as a service charge. Tips are not expected at the food stalls.

TRAVEL & TOURS IN VIETNAM

Vietnam Airlines operate daily flights linking all the major cities. A Saigon to Hanoi return ticket (2-hour flight) costs from £120 (160US$). You must book well in advance during the Tet Festival.
Trains also run regularly between Hanoi and Saigon. A journey on the Reunifica-

WEATHER IN SAIGON

	Jan	Feb	March	April	May	June	July	Aug	Sept	Oct	Nov	Dec
Daytime temperatures in °C/°F												
	32/90	33/91	34/93	35/95	33/91	32/90	31/88	31/88	31/88	31/88	31/88	31/88
Nighttime temperatures in °C/°F												
	21/70	22/72	23/73	24/75	24/75	24/75	24/75	24/75	23/73	23/73	23/73	22/72
Sunshine hours/day												
	5	6	5	6	4	4	4	4	5	4	4	4
Precipitation days/month												
	2	1	2	4	16	21	23	21	21	20	11	7
Water temperature in °C/°F												
	24/75	25/77	25/77	28/82	28/82	28/82	28/82	28/82	28/82	27/81	27/81	25/77

tion Express between north and south is a good way to see the country, but the marathon journey takes 38 hours. Book a 1st class Soft Sleeper ticket and do so well in advance.

Travelling by public overland bus is not advisable, as there have been many serious accidents, especially at night. If you want to travel on a tourist bus, ask in the traveller cafés about Open Tours. The buses, with reclining seats, are new (Hanoi to Hue costs £5/8US$). *Mai Linh Express Bus (tel. in Saigon 08 39 29 29 29)* is a reliable bus company.

A hire car with driver is the time-honoured way for families or small groups to tour the country. Ask for details in your hotel or better still at a travel agency. International car rental companies do not operate in Vietnam. Costs, including driver and petrol, start at approx. £20 (25US$) per day, depending on size of car and distance to be covered. Tourists are not allowed to drive and even riding a moped is officially not permitted (and dangerous).

Mekong Delta tours: *Mekong Eyes Cruise (Can Tho | www.mekongeyes.com)* organise ● boat tours on a converted rice barge with 30 nice double rooms, under German management. Another good tour operator is *Sinh Balo Adventure Travel (283/20 Pham Ngu Lao | Saigon | tel. 08 38 37 67 66 | www.sinhbalo. com | two days for two persons approx. £115/180US$ per person). Tu Trang Travel (www.tutrangtravel.com)* is another company that arranges Mekong Delta tours. If you want luxury travel, then investigate *Pandaw ships*, which run between Saigon/My Tho and Angkor in Cambodia *(www.pandaw.com)*.

VISAS

Tourist visas, issued only by Vietnamese embassies, are valid for up to four weeks and permit a single entry. The cost of a 30-day visa for an independent traveller is £44 (70US$), a fast-track service visa also for 30 days £59 (95US$). To apply for a visa in the UK or the US, check the website of the relevant Vietnamese embassy (see below), where you can download an application form. The normal processing period for a tourist visa is 5 days, but an express service is possible for an extra charge. You must forward your passport, a passport photo and the payment by cheque. Alternatively, you can apply in person. When you arrive in Vietnam, you must fill in an entry form and customs declaration, a duplicate of which must be submitted when you leave.

EMBASSIES OF THE SOCIALIST REPUBLIC OF VIETNAM

– *12 Victoria Road | London W8 5RD | Tel. 020 7937 1912 | http://www.vietnam embassy.org.uk*
– *1233 20th street | NW Suite 400 | Washington, DC 20036 | Tel. 0202 8 61 07 37 | http://vietnamembassy-usa.org*

WEATHER, WHEN TO GO

If you go to the south, then the best time is between December and March, when the temperatures are bearable and there is little rainfall. In April/May, it can be oppressively sultry ahead of the rainy season (from June to December). The months of June to October bring heavy storms and occasionally floods to central Vietnam and the Mekong Delta region. The further north you go, the greater the differences between summer and winter. Whereas sub-tropical summers from April onwards can be hot and humid, from December to February the temperatures on the central/north coast can fall well below 20°C/68°F. In addition, long periods of drizzle can spoil the enjoyment of travel.

USEFUL PHRASES VIETNAMESE

PRONUNCIATION

For ease of pronunciation are all Vietnamese words are provided with a simple pronunciation guide [in square brackets]. The following characters (left column) are special characters and are pronounced as follows (right column):

c	c as in 'cat' mixed with g as in 'go'	ph	ph as in 'phone'	Tones:	
		tr	ch as in 'chip'	a	flat
-ch	ck as in 'lick'	x	s as in 'hiss'	á	high rising like
đ/Đ	d as in 'dog'	â	u as in 'hut'		'day'
d/gi-	z as in 'zip'	e	eah as in 'yeah'	ã	creaky
kh-	ch as in Scottish 'loch'	ê	ay as in 'lay'	à	falling
		ơ	ur	ả	falling, then
ch-	ch as in 'chip'	ú	oo		rising
nh-	ny			ạ	a low 'a-ah'

IN BRIEF	
Yes (according to region)	có [goh]; ừ [ur]; dạ [dya]
No/Maybe	không [kong]/có lẽ [goh lay]
Please/	Xin [seen], Làm ơ n [lahm oin]
Thank you	Cám ỏn [gam un]
Excuse me, please!	Tôi xin lỗi! [toy seen loy]
Pardon?	Xin nhắc lại? [seen nyac lai]
I would like to ...	Tôi muôń ... [toy mu-en]
How much is ...?	Gía bao nhiêu? [zhah bao nyu]
I (don't) like that	Tôi rât/không thích [toy rut/kong thik]
good/bad	tốt [toht]/xâú [sao]
too much/much/little	thât nhiêu [tut nyu]/nhiêù [nyu]/ít [eet]
all/nothing	tâc cả [tuk gah]/không [kong]
Help!	Xin giúp tôi! [seen zyub toy]
ambulance	Xe cứu thương [say kyu tur-ong]
Prohibition/forbidden	câm [gam]
danger/dangerous	nguy hiêm [nyee hem]
May I take your picture?	Tôi đúơc phep chup anh? [toy dur feb dyub an]

GREETINGS, FAREWELL	
Good morning!/afternoon/ Good evening!/night!/Hello!	Xin chào! [seen chao]

BẠN NÓI ĐƯỢC TIẾNG VIỆT KHÔNG?

'Do you speak Vietnamese?' This guide will help you to say the basic words and phrases in Vietnamese

Goodbye!/See you	Chào tạm biệt! [chao tam bee-et]
My name is ...	Tên tôi là ... [tu-en toyla]
What's your name?	Anh/Chị tên gí? [an/chee tu-en zee] (masc/fem)

DATE & TIME

Monday/Tuesday	thứ hai [too hai]/thứ ba [too bah]
Wednesday/Thursday	thứ tư [too du]/thứ năm [too nam]
Friday/Saturday	thứ sáu [too sao]/thứ bảy [too bai]
Sunday	chủ nhật [choo nyut]
holiday/	ngáy nghí [nyai nyee]/
working day	ngáy lam viêc [nyai lahm vee-ek]
today/tomorrow/	hôm này [hom nai]/ngáy may [nyai mai]/
yesterday	hôm qua [hom kwah]
hour/minute	giờ [zur]/phút [phoot]
day/night/week	ngáy [nyai]/đem [daym]/tuần [twun]
What time is it?	Mây giờ rôi? [mai zur roy]
It's three o'clock	Bây giờ là ba giờ [bai-ee zur la bah zur]
It's half past three	Bây giờ la ba mùời [bai-ee zur la bah moy]

TRAVEL

open/closed	mở [mur]/đóng [dong]
entrance/exit	lối vào [loy vao]/lối ra [loy rah]
departure/departure (plane)	khợi hánh [koy hahn]
toilets (ladies/gentlemen)	nhà vê sinh (nử/nam) [nya vay sin (nur/nahm)]
(no) drinking water	(không) nước uống [(kong) nyok wong]
Where is ...?/Where are ...?	ở đâu vây...? [ur duh vay]/ở đâu vây...? [ur duh veh]
left/right	trái [chai]/phải [phai]
straight ahead/back	thăng tới [tang toy]/lui lại [lui lai]
close/far	gân [guhn]/xa [sah]
street map/map	bán đồ [ban doh]
bus/tram/taxi	bus [boos]/táu điên [tao dee-en]/tă'c-xi [taksee]
bus stop	trạm xe bus [chahm say boos]
parking lot	nổi đổ xe [noy doh say]
train station/harbour	nhà ga [nya gah]/bên cảng [ben cang]
airport	sận bay [shun bai]
single/return	đơn giản [don zyan]/tổi vá lúi [toy vah lui]
train / track/platform	táu [tao]/đùóng rây [dur-ong ray]
I would like to rent ...	Tôi muôń thuê ... [toy mu-en too-ay]
a car/a bicycle	ô-tô [otoh]/xe đạp [say dap]
petrol/gas station	trạm xăng đâù [chahm sang dao]

FOOD & DRINK

Could you please book a table for tonight for four?	ông/bà làm ơn cho chúng tôi một bàn bốn người tối nay [ong/bah lahm oin, cho choong toy moh' ban bohn nyu-ay toy nai]
on the terrace	hanh lang [han lang]
by the window	cửa sổ [koo-a soh]
The menu, please	Làm ơn cho tôi thực đơn [lam oin cho toy took doin]
salt/pepper/sugar	muối [moy]/tiêu [tiu]/dừơng [dur-ong]
cold/too salty/ not cooked	lanh [lan]/mặn [mang]/ chưa chín [chu-a chin]
with/without ice	có đá [koh dah]/không có đá [kong koh dah]
fizzy/still	có gas [koh gas]/không có gas [kong koh gas]
vegetarian/allergy	ngưởi ăn chay [noy an chai]/dị ứng [dyay loong]
May I have the bill, please	Làm ơn tính tiền [lam oin, teen dee-en]

SHOPPING

Where can I find ...?	ở đâu có ...? [ur dao goh ...]
pharmacy/chemist	nhà thuốc tây [nya tuok tai]
shopping centre/market	cửa hàng [ku-a hang]/chợ [chur]
kiosk	tạp hóa [tahp hwa]
100 grammes/ 1 kilo	một trăm gram [moht cham gram]/ một kilo [moht kilo]
expensive/cheap	Đặt [dat] / ré [ray]
more/less	nhiêu [nyu]/ít [eet]

ACCOMMODATION

I have booked a room	Tôi có một phòng đả đặt trước [toy goh moh phong dah dut choo]
Do you have any ... left?	ông/bà có còn ...? [ong/bah goh con ...]
single room	phòng đỏn [phong don]
double room	phòng đôi [phong doy]
shower/sit-down bath	Với phòng tăm [voy phong tum]
balcony/terrace	balkon/sân thường [shun tur-ong]

BANKS, MONEY & CREDIT CARDS

bank/ATM	bank [bank] (ngân hàng) [nan hang]/ nồi lấy tiền tự động [noy lay dee-en tu dong]
I'd like to change ...	Tôi muốn đổi ... thành tiền [toy mu-en doy... tan dee-en]
cash/credit card	tiền mặt [dee-en mut]/thẻ tín dụng [tay teen zoong]
change	đổi tiền [doy dee-en]

HEALTH

doctor/dentist/ paediatrician	bắc sĩ [bak shee]/nha sĩ [nya shee]/ bắc sĩ nhi đống [bak shee nyee dong]
hospital	bênh viên [ben vee-en]
fever/pain	sốt [shoht]/đau [dao]
diarrhoea/nausea	tiêu chảy [dee-u chai]/ói mử [oy mur]
inflamed/injured	bị viêm [bee vee-em] / bị thương [bee tur-ong]
plaster/bandage	Cứu th ương cá nhân [kyu tur-ong gah nyun]
pain reliever/tablet	thuốc chóng đau [too-ok chong dao]/Thuốc [too-ok]

POST, TELECOMMUNICATIONS & MEDIA

stamp/letter	tem [tem]/thư [too]
postcard	bưu thiếp [boo tee-ep]
Where can I find internet access?	Nổi truy câp internet? [noy chee gup internet]
socket/adapter/ charger	ổ căm điện [oh gahm dee-en]/biến thế [bee-en tay]/ máy nạp điện [mai nap dee-en]
dial/connection/ engaged	quay số [kwai soh]/nối kêt [noy kurt]/ máy đang bân [mai dan bun]
e-mail address/ internet address (URL)/ at sign (@)	địa chỉ điện tín [dee-a chee dee-en teen]/ địa chỉ điện tín [dee-a chee dee-en teen]/ a còng [ah gong]
internet connection/wifi	Internet/sóng [song]
e-mail/file/print	E-Mail/hộp chửa [hob chua]/in ra [een rah]

LEISURE, SPORTS & BEACH

beach/lido	bải tăm [bai tam]/hố bỏi [hoh boy]
sunshade/lounger	ô [ouh]/ghế bố [gay boh]
low tide/high tide/ current	thưy triều [too-ee chee-oo]/bảo lut [bao lood]/ nưóc chảy [nyok chai]

NUMBERS

0	không [kong]	10	mười [moy]	
1	một [moht]	20	hai mười [hai moy]	
2	hai [hai]	70	bảy mười [bai moy]	
3	ba [bah]	100	một trăm [moht cham]	
4	bốn [bohn]	200	hai trăm [hai cham]	
5	năm [nam]	1000	một ngàn [moht nyan]	
6	sáu [sao]	2000	hai ngàn [hai nyan]	
7	bảy [bai]	10000	mười ngàn [moy nyan]	
8	tám [dahm]	½	một phân hai [moht phan hai]	
9	chín [cheen]	¼	một phân tư [moht phan dur]	

NOTES

ROAD ATLAS

The green line ▬▬ indicates the Trips & Tours (p. 102–107)
The blue line ▬▬ indicates The perfect route (p. 30–31)

All tours are also marked on the pull-out map

Photo: Fishermen near Mui Ne

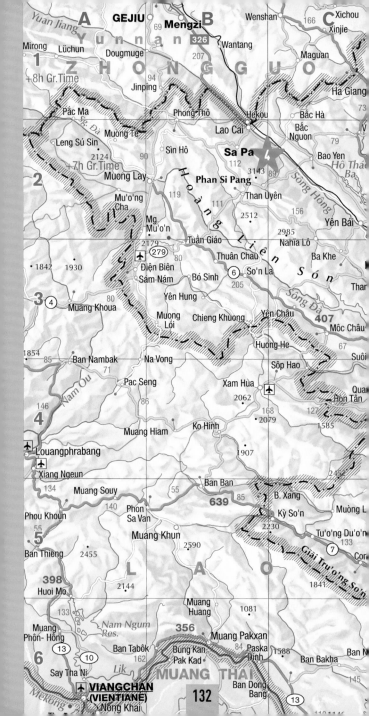

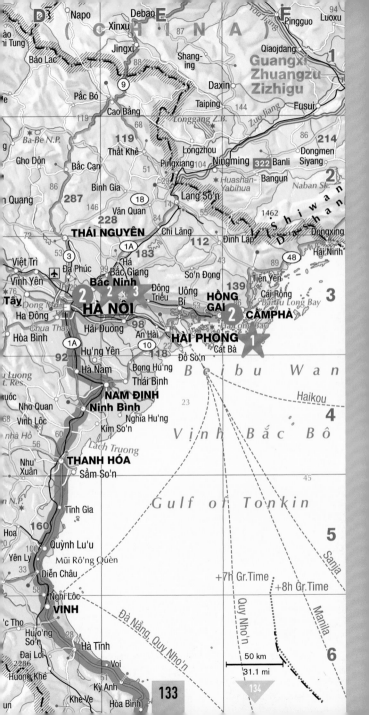

Napo, Debao, Xinxu, Pingguo, Luoxu, You Jiang, 94
C H I N A, F, 1
Jingxi, Shang-ing, Qiaojdang
Guangxi Zhuangzu Zizhigu
ào, Tung, Bảo Lạc, 87, 88
Pắc Bó, 9, Daxin, Taiping, 144, Fusui
Ba-Be N.P., Cao Bằng, 119, 68, Longgang Z.B., Zuo Jiang
119, 86, 214
Thất Khê, Longzhou, Ningming, Banli, Dongmen, Siyang
Gho Dôn, Bắc Cạn, 51, Pingxiang, 104, 322, Bangun, Naban Sk.
86, Bình Gia, 146, Lạng Sơn, 2
Quang, 287, 18, Văn Quan, 84, 55, Huashan-Yabihua, Shiwan
228, Chi Lăng, 14, 1462, Da shan
THÁI NGUYÊN, 183, 112, Đình Lập, Dongxing
Việt Trì, 53, 3, 1A, Hà, 43, 89, 48, Hải Ninh
Đa Phúc, Bắc Giang, Sơn Đông, 139, Tiên Yên
Vĩnh Yên, Bắc Ninh, 99, Đông Triều, Uông Bí, HÔNG GAI, Cái Rồng, Bái Tử Long Bay, 3
Tây, Dong Mo, 2, 2, 3, HÀ NÔI, 98, 53, 36, 2, CÂMPHẢ
76, Chua Thay, Hải Dương, An Hài, HẢI PHÒNG, 22, Hạ Long Bay, 1
Ha Đông, Hòa Bình, 1A, Hư'ng Yên, 10, Cát Bà, Đồ Sơn
92, Hà Nam, Bong Hứ'ng, Thái Bình, B e i b u W a n
Luong, t.Res., Nho Quan, NAM ĐỊNH, Ninh Bình, Nghĩa Hư'ng, 23, Haikou
quôc, 68, Vĩnh Lộc, Kim Sơn, V i n h B ắ c B ô, 4
nhà Hồ, 56, Lach Truong, 45
Nhu' Xuân, THANH HÓA, Sầm Sơn, G u l f o f T o n k i n
N.P., Tĩnh Gia, 5
160, Sanja
Hoa, 100, Quỳnh Lư'u, Mũi Rô'ng Quền
Yên Ly, 33, Diễn Châu, +7h Gr.Time, +8h Gr.Time, Quy Nhơ'n, Manila
58, Nghi Lộc, VINH
c Tho, Hươ'ng Sơ'n, 28, Hà Tĩnh, Đà Nẵng, Quy Nhơ'n, 50 km, 6
Đại Lôi, 2286, Voi, 31.1 mi
Hươ'ng Khê, Kỳ Anh, 133, 134
un, Khê Ve, Hòa Bình

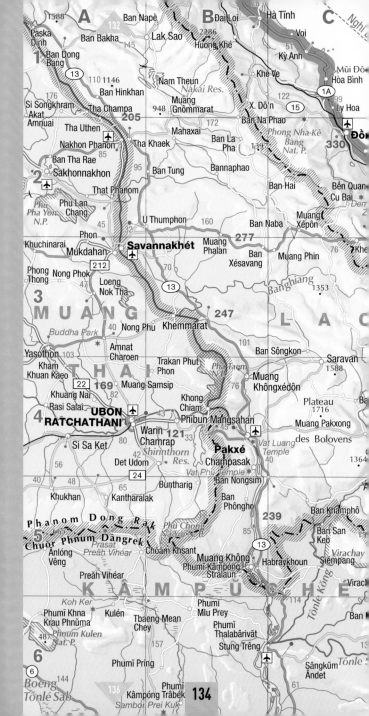

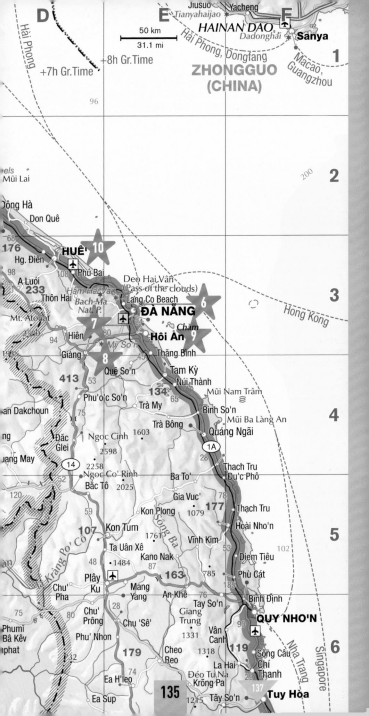

Hải Phòng

Jiusuo Tianyahaijao Yacheng
HAINAN DAO
Hải Phòng, Dongfang Dadonghải Sanya
Macao, Guangzhou

1

+7h Gr.Time +8h Gr.Time

50 km
31.1 mi

ZHONGGUO
(CHINA)

96

els
Mũi Lai

200

2

Đông Hà
Don Quê

~68
176
Hg. Điền
98
A Lưới 108 Phú Bài
233 Thôn Hải
Mt. Atouat Hầm Hải Vân
2500 Bạch Mã Nat. P.
94 Hiên
Giảng

HUẾ **10**

Đèo Hải Vân
(Pass of the clouds)
Lang Co Beach
ĐÀ NẴNG **6**
Cham
HÔI AN **9**
Thăng Bình

Hong Kong

3

7

30

8
Quế So'n
413 53
Phu'o'c So'n
75
Đắc Ngọc Cinh 1603
Glei 2598
uang May 2258
52 Bắc Tô 2025
120

Tam Kỳ
Núi Thành
134 65 Mũi Nam Trâm
Bình So'n
Trà My Mũi Ba Làng An
Trà Bông Quảng Ngãi
1A
28
Thạch Tru
Ba To' Đu'c Phổ

4

an Dakchoun
ng

Krang Po' Cô

107 Kon Tum
48 •1484
Ta Uân Xê Kano Nak
Plây 87
Chu' Ku
Pha Mảng
Chu' Yang
75 Prông 28
80 Phu' Nhon Chu 'Sê'

59 Kon Plong 1761
Gia Vuc' 78
1079 **177**
Vĩnh Kim
Hoài Nho'n
53 Diêm Tiêu
163 •785 Phù Cát
185
An-Khê 76 Bình Định
Tay So'n 90 QUY NHO'N
Giang Vân
Trung Canh
1331

Sông Ba

Thạch Tru

102 **5**

Nha Trang Singapore

Phumi
Bâ Kêv
nphat **179**
732
Ea H'leo
Ea Sup

Cheo 1318
Reo **119** Sông Cầu
La Hai Chí
Đèo Tu Na Thanh
Krông Pa **137** Tuy Hòa
1215 Tây So'n

6

135

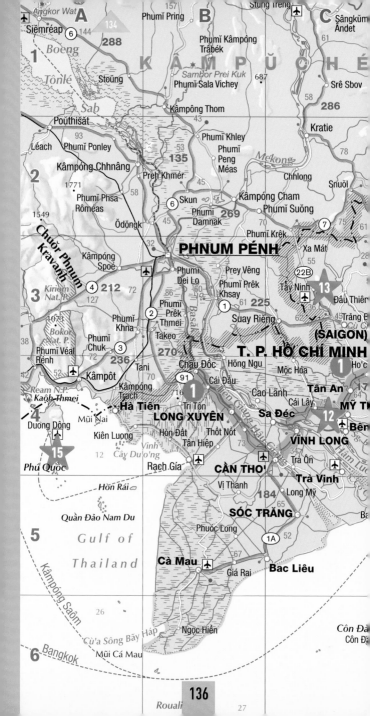

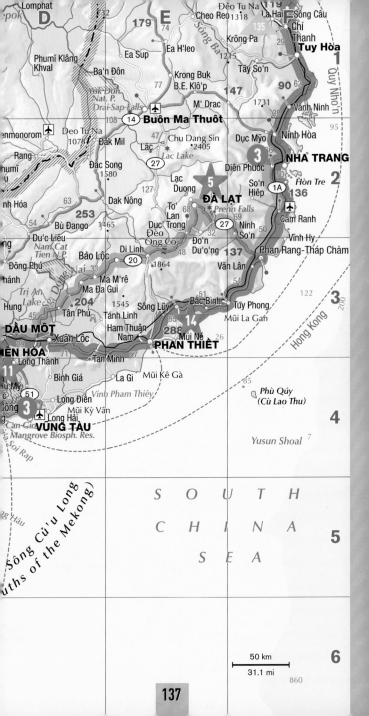

Lomphat

Phumĭ Kbang
Khval

D

732

179

E

Song Ba

Đèo Tu Na 1318
Cheo Reo
Krông Pa
La Hai Sông Cầu
Chí
135
Thanh
29
Tuy Hòa

E

74

Ea Sup

Ea H'leo
Tây So'n

1215

1

Ba'n Đôn

Krong Buk
B.E. Klô'p

147

90

62

Quy Nhơn'n

Rang

enmonorom

Đèo Tu Na
1078

108
14

M' Drac
1731

Vành Ninh

28

95

Đắk Mil

27

47

2405

Ninh Hòa

Đắc Song
1580

Chu Dang Sin

Dục Mỹ

3

NHA TRANG

Lạc
Lạc Lake

Diên Phước

So'n
Hiệp

1A

Hòn Tre

2

136

Dak Nông

Lạc
Duong

ĐÀ LẠT

Prenn Falls

Cam Ranh

127

To'
Lan

68

27

69

Ninh
So'n

50

Vĩnh Hy

Đức Trong

32

Đo'n

Đèo
Ông Cô

48

Du'o'ng

137

Phan Rang-Tháp Chàm

Di Linh

20

1864

Văn Lân

54

122

3

200

Bảo Lộc

Ma M'rê
Ma Đa Gui

Bắc Bình

51

Tuy Phong

Mũi La Gan

Hong Kong

253

Bù Đăng

1465

Du'c Liễu

Nam Cat
Tien N.P.

Đông Phú

hánh

Tri An
Lake

204

Hung

Tân Phú

DẦU MỘT

IÊN HÒA

45

Xuân Lộc

71

29

Long Thành

Tân Phú

1545

Tánh Linh

Ham Thuận
Nam

Sông Lũy

55

14

288

Mũi Né

PHAN THIẾT

26

Tân Minh

57

85

11

ù Mỹ

51

3

Long Điền

Long Hải

Bình Giá

La Gi

Mũi Kê Gà

Vinh Pham Thiêy

Phù Quý
(Cù Lao Thu)

4

ng
g Gió
Soi Rap

VŨNG TÀU

Mũi Kỳ Vân

Mangrove Biosph. Res.

Yusun Shoal

7

ng Hậu

Sông Cử'u Long

uths of the Mekong)

S   O   U   T   H

C   H   I   N   A

S   E   A

5

50 km

31.1 mi

6

860

137

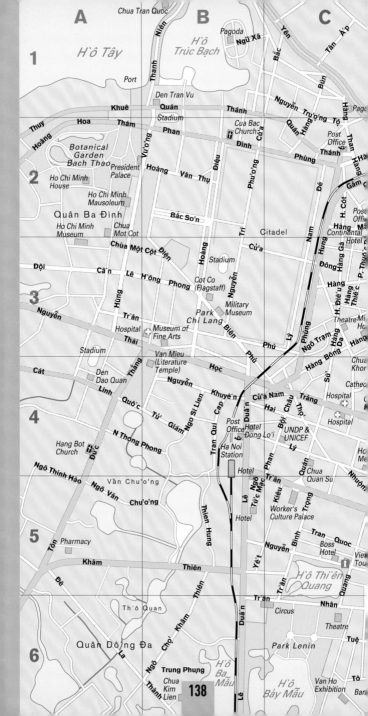

A

1   Hồ Tây   Chua Tran Quoc
Port

Khuê   Quán
Stadium
Thuy   Hoa   Thám   Phan
Hoàng

Botanical
Garden
Bạch Thao
2   Ho Chi Minh   President
House   Palace
Ho Chi Minh
Mausoleum
Quận Ba Đình
Ho Chi Minh   Chua
Museum   Mot Cot
Chùa Một Cột   Điện
Đội   Cần   Lê Hồng Phong
3   Hùng   Trần
Nguyễn
Hospital   Museum of
Thái   Fine Arts
Stadium   Van Mieu
Cát   Den   (Literature
Dao Quan   Temple)
Linh   Nguyễn
Quốc   Tứ   Giám
4   N Thong Phong
Hang Bot   Đức
Church
Ngô Thịnh Hào   Văn Chương
Ngô Văn   Chương
Thien Hung
5   Tôn   Pharmacy
Đê   Khâm   Thiên
Thiên
Thổ Quan
6   Quận Đống Đa   La
Ngô   Chợ   Khâm
Thành   Trung Phụng
Chua Kim Lien

138

B

Pagoda
Ngũ Xã
Hồ
Trúc Bạch

Niên
Thanh
Den Tran Vu
Thành
Cua Bac
Church
Đình
Vương
Hoàng   Văn Thụ   Điệu
Phường
Bắc Sơn
Trí
Cử'a
Hoàng   Stadium
Nguyễn
Cột Cơ
(Flagstaff)
Park   Military
Chi Lang   Museum
Biển
Học
Khuyên
Cấp
Thắng
Tran Qui   Post
Office   Hotel
Đong Lợi
Ha Noi   Đuân
Station
Hotel
Lê   Ngô   Phan
Trúc Mạc
Kiêu
Hotel
Yết
Trân
Thiên   Khâm
Lê
Dươn
Trân
Hồ
Ba
Mẫu
Hồ
Bảy Mẫu
Lê

C

Yên
Bắc
Tân Ấp
Bún
Hàng   Pag
Nguyễn Trường Tộ
Quán   Hàng   Hàng
Post
Office
Phùng   Thành   Than
Hàng
Đê   Gâm
Nam
Hùng
H. Cốt
Post
Offi
Hàng   M
Continental
Hotel
Đông
Hàng Gà
Hàng   H. Điể   P. Thuố
Hàng   Thiệc
Theatre   Mi
Phùng   Hàng   Hồ
Ngõ Trạm   Hàng   Hàng
Phú   Lý   Đã
Hàng Bông
Hàng   Chua
Sử   Khơr
Cử'a Nam   Tràng   Cathe
Hai   Châu   Hospital
Thọ
Bội   UNDP &
Lý   UNICEF
Phan   Ho
Quán   Chua   Me
Trân   Quan Su
Worker's   Nhươn
Culture Palace
Bình   Trân   Quốc
Nguyễn   Trọng
Boss
Hotel
Hồ Thiền   Vie
Quang   Tou
Nhân
Trân
Circus   Theatre
Park Lenin   Tuệ
Van Ho   Tô
Exhibition   Bar

D   **E**   **F**

Biên

Long

Cầu

1

Huyện Gia Lâm

Bus
Station

Ái Mỗ

Nguyễn Văn Cừ

Trần

Xuan

Nhật

Boutique

Chiếu

Phúc

Nguyễn Siêu

Chua Bach Ma

Duy Tân

Cầu

Chương

Dương

2

2

Phú Viên

Hàng

Bưởm

Hàng

H. Đạo

Hàng

Röhrenhaus

Mã Mây

Nguyễn

Hữu Huân

Bắc

Trần

Sông

Hồng

Gia Ngư'

Cầu Gỗ

Đình

H. Thùng

Bạch

Port

3

Đền
Ngọc Son

Lê

Water
Puppetry
Theatre

Quân Hoàn Kiểm

Hồ
Hoàn
Kiểm

hua

Da

Thái

Tô'

2

Tiền

Hoàng

Trần Nguyễn Hản

Bank Culture
House

Park I.
Gandhi

Nguyễn

Quyền

Tong

Quang

Khải

National
Bank

4

Thi

Hàng
Khay

Bại

Tràng

Trần

General
Post Office

Hotel
Sofitel
Metropole

Tiền
Trinh

Đạn

Le Bon
Café

Museum of
Revolution

Historical
Museum

Pham

Bà

Museum of
Women

u'ong

Trưng

Opera

Lê

Geological
Museum

Trần

Đảng

Police

Vietnam
Tourism

Chu

Kiệt

Thánh

Ngu Lao

5

Hưng

Hàng

Ngô

Phan

Lò

Đạo

Trần

Restaurant
AuLac House

Hang

Hospital

Khánh

an

st
ice

Youth
Theatre

Thánh

Ton

Theatre

Mã

Chuoi

Huu Nghi
Hospital

Ha Noi

500 m

547 yd

6

Hoà

Pharmacy

Service

Nguyễn

Công

Đức

Trú

Tong

Dư

inh

Huê

Quân Hai Bà Trư'ng

Đền Hai
Ba Trung

139

KEY TO ROAD ATLAS

Autobahn, mehrspurige Straße - in Bau Highway, multilane divided road - under construction	═══ ══ ══	Autoroute, route à plusieurs voies - en construction Autosnelweg, weg met meer rijstroken - in aanleg
Fernverkehrsstraße - in Bau Trunk road - under construction	─── ── ──	Route à grande circulation - en construction Weg voor interlokaal verkeer - in aanleg
Hauptstraße Principal highway	─────────	Route principale Hoofdweg
Nebenstraße Secondary road	·············	Route secondaire Overige verharde wegen
Fahrweg, Piste Practicable road, track	·············	Chemin carrossable, piste Weg, piste
Straßennummerierung Road numbering	E20 11 70 26 5 40 9	Numérotage des routes Wegnummering
Entfernungen in Kilometer Distances in kilometers	259 130 129	Distances en kilomètres Afstand in kilometers
Höhe in Meter - Pass Height in meters - Pass	1365 •	Altitude en mètres - Col Hoogte in meters - Pas
Eisenbahn - Eisenbahnfähre Railway - Railway ferry	▬▬▬▬ ··········	Chemin de fer - Ferry-boat Spoorweg - Spoorpont
Autofähre - Schifffahrtslinie Car ferry - Shipping route		Bac autos - Ligne maritime Autoveer - Scheepvaartlijn
Wichtiger internationaler Flughafen - Flughafen Major international airport - Airport	✈ ✈	Aéroport importante international - Aéroport Belangrijke internationale luchthaven - Luchthaven
Internationale Grenze - Provinzgrenze International boundary - Province boundary	▨▨▨▨▨▨	Frontière internationale - Limite de Province Internationale grens - Provinciale grens
Unbestimmte Grenze Undefined boundary	▨▨ ─ ▨▨ ─	Frontière d'Etat non définie Rijksgrens onbepaalt
Zeitzonengrenze Time zone boundary	-4h Greenwich Time ········ -3h Greenwich Time	Limite de fuseau horaire Tijdzone-grens
Hauptstadt eines souveränen Staates National capital	**MANILA**	Capitale nationale Hoofdstad van een souvereine staat
Hauptstadt eines Bundesstaates Federal capital	**Kuching**	Capitale d'un état fédéral Hoofdstad van een deelstat
Sperrgebiet Restricted area	▭▭▭▭	Zone interdite Verboden gebied
Nationalpark National park	▭▭▭▭	Parc national Nationaal park
Antikes Baudenkmal Ancient monument	∴	Monument antiques Antiek monument
Sehenswertes Kulturdenkmal Interesting cultural monument	*Angkor Wat*	Monument culturel interéssant Bezienswaardig cultuurmonument
Sehenswertes Naturdenkmal Interesting natural monument	*Ha Long Bay*	Monument naturel interéssant Bezienswaardig natuurmonument
Brunnen Well	◡	Puits Bron
Ausflüge & Touren Trips & Tours	▬▬▬▬	Excursions & tours Uitstapjes & tours
Perfekte Route Perfect route	▬▬▬▬	Itinéraire idéal Perfecte route
MARCO POLO Highlight	★1	MARCO POLO Highlight

INDEX

This index lists all sights, museums and destinations plus the main squares and streets, the key terms and people featured in this guide. Numbers in bold indicate a main entry

WRITE TO US

e-mail: info@marcopologuides.co.uk

Did you have a great holiday?
Is there something on your mind?
Whatever it is, let us know!
Whether you want to praise, alert us
to errors or give us a personal tip –
MARCO POLO would be pleased to
hear from you.
We do everything we can to provide
the very latest information for your trip.

Nevertheless, despite all of our authors'
thorough research, errors can creep
in. MARCO POLO does not accept any
liability for this. Please contact us by
e-mail or post.

MARCO POLO Travel Publishing Ltd
Pinewood, Chineham Business Park
Crockford Lane, Chineham
Basingstoke, Hampshire RG24 8AL
United Kingdom

PICTURE CREDITS
Cover Photograph: Na Thrang, Xom Bong bridge (Getty Images/Robert Harding World Imagery: Francis)
Photos: DuMont Bildarchiv: Krause (34, 70, 75, 82, 101, 113, 114/115, 119); Getty Images/Robert Harding World Imagery: Francis (1 top); Global Surf Industries (16 bottom); Huber: Damm (2 bottom, 54/55), Gräfenhain (10/11, 37, 41), Picture Finders (23); F. Ihlow (27, 42, 65); iStockphoto.com: redmonkey8 (16 top); Laif: Selbach (104); MAI GALLERY: Nguyen Anh Tuan (17 top); mauritius images: Kugler (61); M. Miethig (1 bottom); Minh Hanh: Hai Dong (16 centre); Mosaique Decoration: Ha Thuc Phu Nam (17 bottom); D. Renckhoff (59, 112); T. Stankiewicz (2 top, 5, 6, 30 l., 63, 87); M. Weigt (flap l., 2 centre top, 2 centre bottom, 3 centre, 3 bottom, 4, 7, 8, 9, 12/13, 15, 18/19, 20, 24/25, 26 l., 26 r., 28, 28/29, 29, 30 r., 32/33, 38, 44, 46, 49, 51, 53, 56, 60, 66, 67, 69, 72, 76/77, 78, 81, 84, 89, 92, 93, 95, 96, 98/99, 102/103, 106, 107, 108/109, 110/111, 112/113, 114, 115, 118 top, 118 bottom, 130/131); White Star: Schiefer (flap r., 91)

1st Edition 2013
Worldwide Distribution: Marco Polo Travel Publishing Ltd, Pinewood, Chineham Business Park,
Crockford Lane, Basingstoke, Hampshire RG24 8AL, United Kingdom. Email: sales@marcopolouk.com
© MAIRDUMONT GmbH & Co. KG, Ostfildern
Chief editors: Michaela Lienemann (concept, managing editor), Marion Zorn (concept, text editor)
Author: Wolfgang Veit; Co-author: Martina Miethig; Editor: Petra Klose
Programme supervision: Anita Dahlinger, Ann-Katrin Kutzner, Nikolai Michaelis
Picture editor: Gabriele Forst
What's hot: wunder media, Munich;
Cartography road atlas: © MAIRDUMONT, Ostfildern; Cartography pull-out map: © MAIRDUMONT, Ostfildern
Design: milchhof : atelier, Berlin; Front cover, pull-out map cover, page 1: factor product munich
Translated from German by Paul Fletcher, Suffolk; editor of the English edition: Tony Halliday, Oxford
Prepress: BW-Medien GmbH, Leonberg
Phrase book in cooperation with Ernst Klett Sprachen GmbH, Stuttgart, Editorial by Pons Wörterbücher

DOS & DON'TS

A few things to bear in mind in Vietnam

DON'T TOUCH THE MONKS

Orthodox Buddhists abide strictly by the rule that no woman may touch them. If this happens to a monk, he has to carry out time-consuming cleansing rituals, because he is deemed to have become 'unclean'. If you would like to present a gift to a monk, the best way to do this is via someone familiar with the etiquette, a tour guide, for example. Also, wait to be offered a hand to shake – if a monk does not offer you his hand, do not under any circumstances take the initiative.

DON'T GIVE TO BEGGARS

Even if they arouse your compassion, do not give money to street beggars. In Saigon alone, there are thousands of professional beggars often organised into rings and exploited by unscrupulous racketeers, with many thousands more throughout the rest of the country. They are only interested in cash. As a tourist, you are advised not to give spare change to the many poor people you will see on your travels. Instead, donate your money to one of the charitable organisations that cares for street children and the disabled, such as *Saigon Children (www.saigonchildren.com)*, *Reaching Out (www.reachingoutvietnam.com)* in Hoi An or the *Hoa Sua School (www.hoasuaschool.com)* in Sapa. For more information, visit *Terre des Hommes (www.terredeshommes.org)*.

DON'T SHOW OFF

The Vietnamese are reserved people, not least because of their exposure to Confucian philosophy. Do not boast about your success or your income or parade status symbols in front of the locals, nor should you sing the praises of your home country. Nobody will be impressed.

AVOID TRAVELLING AT THE TIME OF THE TET FESTIVAL

At Tet, Vietnamese New Year, the whole of Vietnam and millions of expatriate Vietnamese are on the move. Tours and tickets – if any are available – can be up to 50 percent more expensive. Rooms suddenly cost double the normal rate, public services and tours are paralysed for a week and many restaurants and shops close.

DO COMPLY WITH THE SOCIAL NORMS

In Vietnam, strength lies in inner peace. You are on holiday, so don't rush things. Whatever it is you are waiting for will eventually happen. If you get excited, if you make a fuss about everyday events and break Confucian rules, you are showing that you have lost control of your inner self and therefore you do not deserve respect. Whatever the reason, nothing could be worse – whether you're wearing unsuitable clothing in a temple, sunbathing in the nude, kissing in public, showing impatience, even sweating excessively.